A LIFE IN LINCOLNSHIRE TITLE— NUMBER ELEVEN

MY DAD AND I

MY DAD AND I

by

HANNAH MARJORAM

Illustrated by

DAVID CLENCH

1970  1994

RICHARD KAY
80 SLEAFORD ROAD • BOSTON • LINCOLNSHIRE • PE21 8EU

The right of Doreen Rowland to be identified as the author of the text
of this work has been asserted by her in accordance with the provisions
of The Copyright Designs and Patents Act 1988.
   The right of David Clench to be identified as the creator of the
illustrations in this work has been asserted by him in accordance with
the requirements of the Copyright, Design and Patents Act 1988.

© Doreen Rowland 1994 (text)
© David Clench 1994 (illustrations)

ISBN 0 902662 19 8 (cased edition)
ISBN 0 902662 29 5 (paperback edition)

Typeset on an AppleMacintosh computer using Microsoft Word and
PageMaker applications and reproduced initially by means of a
LaserWriter Plus laserprinter.

Printed by Woolnough Bookbinding Ltd.,
Express Works, Church Street, IRTHLINGBOROUGH, Northants. NN9 5SE

For my family
PETER, ANTONY AND JUDY

CONTENTS

ILLUSTRATIONS

1.

At the Age of Four . . .

HE DAY WAS GOD-GIVEN. High above me a lark trilled and twirled; etched against the sky the chestnut tree stood, hazy in the afternoon sunshine, its white candles gleaming in glory. Beneath its branches the cattle, grateful for the shade, twitched their tails, too lazy even to crop the leaves within reach.

I scuffed my feet in the dust and watched the particles re-settle on my legs and shoes; a somnolent fly flew away, then returned to its place on my knee. The cat, draped against my arm, moved a fraction and kneaded its way closer into my side; sighed deeply and drifted off to sleep again. Wisps of cotton-wool cloud floated silently across the innocent sky and all was quiet; even the lark, satisfied that it had made its point, drifted into anonymity. The sharp scent of young nettles vied with the perfume of the meadowsweet in the hedgerow. All was peace.

The faint bleat of distant lambs failed to probe my awareness; the drone of an occasional bee, in replete satisfaction, passed un-noticed. Suddenly a hen burst forth from its nettle hideaway cackling in triumph at the day's duty safely accomplished. She paused once to glance at me, then strutted away, beady eyes satisfied. Busily, she pecked among the bright grass as if the five o'clock feed was no more a certainty today than it was any other day of the week. Silence again, but my skin of consciousness had been pierced; my time of stillness ruptured, and the day returned to its normal pace. But my moment of heightened awareness had been encapsulated in a fraction of time, to be savoured again in middle age when the edge of one's senses is less finely honed, or when needed to lift the spirit in times of trouble. The experience was forever mine.

A wet nose prodded my arm as the collie nuzzled me into activity. I scrambled to my feet, the cat still dangling over my arm, and followed the dog from the field and along the yard. Leaving the bright light behind, I entered the restful shade of the kitchen and found my mother sitting quietly in her chair, enjoying a few unaccustomed minutes of rest. She opened her eyes and smiled at me and I, lost for words, just stared at her. How could a four-year-old find the right way to say 'Thank you' for the most wonderful birthday present of her life? I looked down at my crimson silk blouse with incredulous eyes, then stared at my mother again. She smiled at me with complete understanding: I was so happy.

Not that one can always recognise happiness at the time: it's just that life seems . . . acceptable. I used to wander in the fields looking for rabbits; my favourite food was roast rabbit and I was, always hopefully, trying to catch one. My Dad used to laugh at me and told me that all I had to do was to put salt on their tails. So I carefully poured salt into a screw of kitchen paper and sallied forth. Our farm was not large and every field had a name. Collectively the fields to the east of the farmyard were called 'The Levels'; why I'll never know unless perhaps it was because of the obvious – that they were quite flat. Then there were the 'Top Fields' up above the railway line, and finally the 'Home Field' which is self-explanatory. Within these groupings there were individual names: one small grass enclosure was delightfully known as 'The Pingles'.

I always went rabbit-hunting down the Levels. The beck which ran through the farm meandered its way through those fields and the rabbits had huge warrens along its banks – much to my dad's disgust. I spent hours sitting like a statue waiting for the rabbits to play far enough away from their burrows to give me a chance to edge myself between them and their holes. When such an opportunity presented itself I ran as fast as my four-year-old legs would carry me, salt at the ready to annoint their tails as they scurried to their homes. Needless to say, I was never successful; I had to rely on the ferrets or on my dad's twelve-bore shotgun to supply the rabbit dinners.

One of my favourite pastimes was walking with my dad to feed the chickens and collect the eggs. As I was small I wriggled through the chickens' hatch and handed out the eggs to be put into the bucket which had contained their food. This saved opening the big door into the hen-house. Mother used to be pretty scathing about the state of my clothing when I arrived back. If the hens were broody they disliked having their eggs removed so I had to reach under them to steal their eggs. They took great exception to this and pecked my arms thoroughly as well as swearing at me. I soon learnt to wear long sleeves for this job.

One day we went into one of the Top Fields to look at the poultry there. It was a lovely summer morning, already quite hot with a hint of haze. As I passed a rotten, fallen tree my dad suddenly dropped the bucket of food, pushed me away and jumped forward into the tufty grass by the base of the tree. He then stamped about frantically for a few seconds, finally pausing to move me away again to shorter grass. I peered round him to see what all the fuss was about. On the broken area was a very sad and sorry-looking, broken snake – an adder. Apparently as I had danced along at Dad's side I had all but trodden on it. What a blessing that the farmers in those days wore leggings! These were black leather tubes buckled round the legs and stretched from ankle to just below the knee. It was a point of honour on market day to have them blacked and buffed up until they gleamed. They were obviously snake-proof!

When Dad first began to farm he was in partnership with his brother. Their father gave them £300 and all his old implements to start with, so life was no bed of roses. Although they were the best of friends, after three or four years they decided each to go his own way. So Uncle Sid, bought out by my dad, moved to a farm going cheap for tenancy about two and a half miles away. They continued to help each other out with both implements and labour.

Family lore contains a number of incidents about my Dad at this time. Two are worth re-telling here. The first concerns a day when Uncle came over to Asgarby to borrow the seed drill, riding on a cart horse that would pull the drill back to his farm.

3.

He arrived during the early afternoon and went into the stackyard to arrange the transaction. Then, yoking his horse to the drill, he prepared to return home. At that point he realised that he had not seen my mother, so off he went to the farmhouse to pass the time of day. At that time my two older brothers were in their infancy: Frank was a tiny baby in his cot, and Raymond – known to all as Ray – was a toddler of about three. Mum and Uncle duly exchanged pleasantries and enjoyed a pot of tea until Uncle made tracks for home. He unhitched his horse, turned it round, sat on the back of the shafts and set off. Some forty-five minutes later, as Uncle turned the horse into the lane leading to his own farm, he glanced behind him and to his horror saw that little Ray had followed him on his tiny legs all the way behind the drill. Full of consternation, he tied up the horse, picked Ray up, carried him into the house and sat him down at the kitchen table. Out came the bread and jam, and after brewing another pot of tea, Uncle sat down as well and decided to make a meal of it. Little Ray seemed quite content that Uncle should feed him before taking him home!

However, back at Asgarby, Mother was more than a trifle worried. She hadn't missed him to begin with; she thought he was safely at play in the 'causey', the small walled enclosure by the kitchen door. When she found he was not there, she searched the house, the garden and orchard, the sheds, the calf boxes and the chicken huts. Now she did begin to worry; she ran to the big pond in Home Field – no body there, thank goodness. What about the Levels Pond? A quick dash there and still no Ray. He wasn't in the beck, nor in the dog's kennel. Now really frightened, she ran to the Top Field where my dad was harrowing the land and poured out her trouble. Dad, with both his men, searched every inch of the place. Then they remembered Uncle Sid's visit, so Dad set off on his bicycle for Ewerby to see if Uncle had noticed him. Imagine Dad's relief when he dashed into Uncle's kitchen and found the pair of them, tucking into a good farmhouse tea. In fact it looked so good that Dad drew up a chair and joined them; after all, he felt rather peckish after all his exertions! It was some time before Ray was placed on the crossbar of Dad's bicycle and pedalled gently home

in the growing dusk. My mother was relieved, angry, tearful and absolutely furious! And I'm not sure that Dad ever understood quite why.

The second incident also involved Ray who was certainly no angel but at that tender age his mischief was of the careless variety – just not bothering to do as he was told. One day, my mother took him and baby Frank down to the Levels with her to feed the chickens. I don't know what his crime was that day but he exasperated Mother to such an extent that she picked him up and spanked him. In fact she lathered him with such gusto that her wedding ring flew off her work-thinned fingers and spun into the tufty grass some distance away. She put Ray down and walked across to the grass where she expected to bend down and pick up the ring at once. She didn't! She searched for ages, growing more and more tearful as time went by, but still she could not find the missing ring. She marked the spot, and after tea Dad came down with her and they really turned every blade of grass over but with no luck: the ring was never found.

Dad promised that he would replace it, but the time went by and my mother could never actually pin him down to parting with money that might otherwise buy food, or livestock or tools. After all, it was a question of priorities, and Dad would have to lay out the equivalent of at least half a calf! Mother became so embarrassed that when she went to Church to take Communion she'd put her engagement ring on and turn it over, plain side up. However, when she went shopping she was usually in too much of a rush to remember to do that, so when she removed her gloves to handle the money from her purse she received some very old-fashioned looks, particularly as she was accompanied by three young children. That was nothing, however, compared with the ribald comments of the market stall-holders! When her mother died some six years later, she asked for – and got from her father – her mother's wedding ring which she wore for the rest of her life. I guess my dad thought he was in no danger of losing her!

2.

MY FAMILY AND FRIENDS

AS I WAS THE YOUNGEST of the family I couldn't wait to grow old enough to go to school. At long last the day arrived and I was dressed in hand-knitted jumper and skirt, socks and little boots; then to my disgust an apron in order to keep my clothes clean. The final indignity was a handkerchief pinned to the chest of my apron! I had my sandwiches and an apple in a small tin and off I set, with the boys, to catch the bus. I was deposited at the next village while they went on to the big school in the neighbouring market town of Sleaford.

I soon found one or two like-minded spirits to make friends with and settled down very quickly. Looking back, I now realise this was because of the expertise of my teacher, Miss Revill who, though a 'student teacher' – i.e. unqualified – was a natural at the job. We twenty or so infants were herded into a small room with a large, open fire, well-guarded, and sat at desks built in banks of four with tip-up seats. These led to much horse-play because if one seat went up, they all went up!

For arithmetic lessons we shared an abacus, one between two. Now these were wooden frames with wires strung across and different coloured, wooden beads on each, which you whizzed back and forth according to the numbers Miss asked you for. Unfortunately I'd been taught to count and knew my numbers before going to school so, much to my disgust, I was moved up from the baby class within the week. How I yearned for those coloured beads going 'ping' across their wires! For writing, we were given slates and chalk. These slates had painted white lines so that we could get the capital and lower-case letters exactly the right height. The hours we spent at those slates, grinding the chalk down and trying to stop the searing squeak which went right through you!

We always ended the day with Miss reading a story to us. Everyone's favourite involved Brer Rabbit in some form or other.

On Friday afternoons Miss Revill finished by opening her bag, taking out a big bar of chocolate, breaking it into squares and every child collected a square as he or she went out and said 'Goodnight'. We all looked forward to that. To her eternal credit, Miss Revill never threatened to deprive us of that treat, however naughty we had been. How she managed to afford it for us all from her tiny wage I'll never know! She lived with her parents in the Rectory gardener's cottage – a 'two-up and two-down' – together with her sister who was dying of TB, and her brother. About two years after her sister died, her brother was killed in a flying accident early in World War Two: the phrase 'There's no justice' comes to mind.

Play and dinner times were eagerly awaited, the girls all herded together on one side of the playground while the boys went about their various concerns on the other. Now down one side of the play ground was a row of four closets which need no other description than that the Powers that Be were always going to build us some new ones that had water, but never did. The boys were allocated two, and so were the girls. One day we thought there was a suspicious amount of giggling going on among the boys and though dying to know the joke we stuck our little noses in the air – 'See if we care about your silly stories!' At afternoon play, two small girls went over to their closets and shut the doors. Suddenly, one agonised scream was followed by another and two red-faced, furious girls erupted through the doors, knickers round their knees, looking for boys to kill! Apparently, some of the lads had prised away a brick in the back of each lavatory; had acquired a longish elder twig which they poked in through the gap and tickled the girls' bottoms as soon as they sat down!

This was a Church of England school and every week the local vicar came along for prayers and the scripture lesson. It was like a direct contact with God: with his flowing white beard the Vicar was just like the picture of the Almighty in the front of the big Bible. Old habits die hard, and if the Vicar passed by in  his pony and trap while we were all walking along the road to catch the bus, the girls all curtsied and the boys touched their caps. When I mentioned this to my dad, he was furious! 'Who does he think he is', he thundered from the stance of his Chapel upbringing, 'he's not the Lord!' Thereafter, I was forbidden to curtsey as we were all equal in the sight of God. At first I turned away and pretended not to see him, but eventually I had the courage to stand my ground and give him a friendly wave. I thought I'd better keep in with him – just in case he *was* God!

Dad had some twenty or so cows. He sold most of the milk; some was put through the separator to extract the cream for butter-making, while the separated milk was used to feed the calves and the pigs. The milk for household use was sold wholesale to a roundsman in the next village. He had a pony and cart, and rejoiced in the name of Mr Cod. Of course he was always known as 'Coddy' to us children. It seems difficult to believe but, at the time we took milk to Mr Cod, we had a waggoner called Billy Onion, a labourer called Leek, and, later, a lad helping to harvest named Jim Bacon.

Our most stalwart employee at that time though was a labourer called 'Owd Sam'. He gave his all to us for thirty-two shillings a week. Of course he had his tied cottage, free skimmed milk, and a large garden where he kept a fat pig and some chickens. He was one of the old school, seemingly content with his lot and always referring to my father as 'T' Maister'. A favourite phrase of his came at the end of the day when he volunteered to take 'yon hosses t' cloase ter git watter'. I suppose his forbears had always talked of a 'close' instead of a field from the time of the enclosures. Owd Sam never had a watch; he took it for granted that he would work from dawn to dusk – and always did!

Another character – of quite a different kind – was our New Forest pony known as Tommy. His main role in life was to pull the milk-float every morning down to Mr Cod, but Tommy had a

sense of humour and it seemed to us children that he had the endearing and delightful ability to laugh at his own jokes. He had several party tricks – for example, he could undo nearly any gate. He learnt to lift up snecks with his nose, to chew through twine or string, and if these measures failed he merely turned round and pushed with his ample rump until something – whether gate, post, or adjoining hedge – gave way. Then he'd go walkabout!

Some mornings he'd be waiting by the stable door for his harness and float, all ready to go. Other mornings, he'd go for a trot down the lanes and we'd scatter in all directions looking for him. Sometimes he'd wait angelically by the Home Field gate, then when Dad was one step away he'd flick up his heels and circle the field as much as to say, 'Come on, catch me'. One of his special games was calculated to make my father see red. He would trot along in the shafts of the milk-float, wait while the churns were unloaded and then, just as Dad turned to bid farewell to Mr Cod, Tommy would take off – straight back to the farm without waiting for the driver!

When I was about four, my two brothers and I walked down to the Levels on some game or other when we came across Tommy in a field where he had no right to be. So as a punishment we decided all three would ride him back to his allotted pasture! We took him to a fence, Frank and Ray held him by the mane while I climbed the fence and clambered onto his back. Then Frank followed suit to sit behind me. Now came the tricky part: Ray let go his mane and in turn just managed to balance himself on the pony's rump. Tommy was as good as gold, standing perfectly still. As soon as we were all settled, clinging tightly one behind the other, he very carefully reared up and gently slid us all off,

11.

one after the other, into a heap in the dyke bottom. That was when he turned round and laughed at us!

Whenever my dad had to leave the farm to go to a neighbouring town or village, I was always around, waiting to be lifted into the trap, absolutely certain that he'd take me. He never used my given name for many years; to him I was always Babster.

Now Babster was in seventh heaven when the time came round for visiting the mill in Heckington. We would trot along in the trap, Tommy tripping along at a fair pace, his little shoes every now and again striking sparks from the stones in the road. Of course the sun was shining – it always did! When we arrived, the sacks of corn would be lifted down and taken to be milled into meal for the calves and chickens, and I was left to wander at will. I loved the groaning, creaking sounds of the massive sails swinging round; I loved the smell of the corn, I even loved the feel of the dust as it settled on my face and hair.

Business done, we'd mount the trap again and set off, down the village street until we came to a tiny cottage set back in its own little garden with a small, wooden lean-to against the side wall. Dad and I would go along the old, brick-edged path and rap on the door. Eventually, it would be opened by an elderly lady who actually wore a Victorian cap on her head. We were always invited in to their tiny kitchen-cum-living room for this was the home of Mr and Miss Stubley. Mr Stubley was the village cobbler; he was a first-rate craftsman, and the repaired boots and shoes always left his hands looking like new. He had one great handicap – he was deaf and dumb. At least, he was stone deaf from birth and presumably couldn't speak because he'd never heard speech. However, his sister was adept at talking to him with her fingers and he was equally adept at answering. They were a lovely, kind couple and everyone was very fond of them. Miss Stubley loved children and kept a bag of sweets on the table for any who happened along. They were genuine, gentle folk.

Leaving the Stubleys, we would trot home, and usually Dad would allow me to drive once we were away from the houses. I took great pride in telling Tommy to 'Gee-up' and clicking my tongue at him. He would flick his chestnut ears and I could almost hear him thinking, 'This is a change of driver, better be careful with her!' So although I thought I was driving Tommy home, he obviously thought he was in charge.

Usually Dad was very easy going with the children and left the discipline to Mother, but occasionally one of us would rile him to such an extent that he'd grab the first thing that came to hand and mete out punishment. From Mother, the normal retribution was a box on the ear; short, sharp and to the point, with no lasting resentment on our part – we knew we deserved it. I do remember though, on a few occasions, when I was very small being told by my mother, 'If you don't do as you're told Boney will get you!' I couldn't think who this beastly man Boney was – it bothered me for years. I think I must have been one of the last children in the country to have been frightened by the threat of Napoleon Bonaparte. Sayings die hard – deep in the country.

One day the boys suffered an unusual form of punishment. They used to sleep together in a big, brass-railed, double bed directly over the kitchen. This room had the only wooden floor in the house and as the boards were placed flush over the beams in the kitchen ceiling, sound penetrated quite easily – both ways. Like all brothers, Frank and Ray were always squabbling. As they were so close in age they fought for supremacy and this rivalry continued at bedtime in no uncertain way, the chief bone of contention being which of them had the bigger half of the bed. As the bed was very old and the springing virtually non-existent, the boys usually ended up in a heap in the middle unless they had the sense to grab the side of the bed and hang on. Mother didn't appreciate this, for when she made the bed in the morning with no weight on it, it looked flat enough.

However, every night the thumps and bumps and shouts and cries carried on until my parents' patience gave out. Then one of them would get the carving fork out of the kitchen drawer and with the handle end, bang on the beam above their head. Then they'd threaten the boys and order silence. There would follow a temporary truce, but shortly another thump would announce that one of them had been shoved out of bed again. My parents could always tell which one it was: if the gun-rack rocked on the wall it was Frank's side; if the stag's antlers shivered Ray had hit the floor.

One night they had been sent to bed early for some misdemeanour. After much squabbling and repeated warnings, mother could stand it no longer. She stood up, reached for a tea towel, and wrapping it round her hand she marched out to the orchard. There she stooped down and plucked a bunch of long nettles . . . back into the house, determination written in every line, up the stairs and flung open the door of the boys' room. To their utter astonishment, bedclothes were stripped off; pyjama trousers whipped down leaving exposed two bare bottoms. Mother then applied the nettles! Horrified silence ensued for a moment, then anguished cries and yells of rage and pain. Mother said not a word, merely held up the bunch of nettles. Back downstairs, all that could be heard were muffled snuffles; not a bump, nor thump, nor crash. Once again, the house curled asleep round our family.

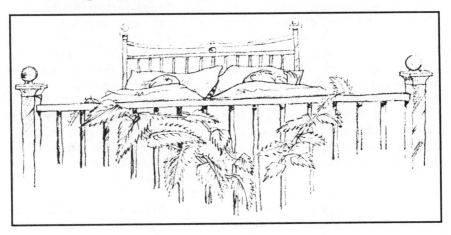

3.

DAD AND HIS ANIMALS

APART FROM MOTHER'S HOUSE-CAT, a Manx who rejoiced for obvious reasons in the name of Stump, the only other really favoured animal was Jim, the Collie, who was Dad's right hand with the sheep. He was also Dad's shadow whenever he was in the yard. Only in the most extreme bad weather did Jim come into the house when he would disappear from sight under the kitchen table to lie across Dad's feet. He was well-hidden there, for straight away after the mid-day meal Mother put a red chenille cloth, with bobbles round the edge, over the table – then put the brass lamp in the centre. This simple action transformed the working kitchen into the working living room. There were three Windsor chairs and a stool round the kitchen range, and a hand-made snip rug on the floor; all very warm and cosy on a winter's evening.

I'm sure this part of the house had altered very little over the last two hundred years or so. There was an enormous bread oven to one side of the hearth and on the other a brewing copper where the farmers of yesteryear brewed the October ale for the men. The range with oven and side-boiler was set back into a great open hearth where the spit attachments were still visible. The floor was made of twelve inch square bricks laid directly on the earth; some were so worn through the traffic of feet over the centuries that there were sunken pathways from the back door to the hearth and another across to the big dairy. The ceiling had one huge oak beam right across and smaller transverse beams leading from it to the side walls. On these smaller beams were large iron hooks which, when let down, held the bacon drying racks in place.

Over in one corner by the brewing copper a ladder led up to a trapdoor in the ceiling; this gave access to the loft where the hired men slept in the old times – no going up the staircase for them! Unless the weather was diabolical the kitchen door was always propped open, probably to gain extra light in the place. And that was Jim's self-appointed place – the kitchen doorway. He would lie full length across it so that everyone, coming in or going out, had to step right over him. We were all so used to it that we did it without thinking – in fact I've seen Mother automatically step over him when he was not there!

Every second Sunday we visited my dad's parents. It was a special occasion; we used the car! They lived in a village about ten miles away and we would set off as soon as Sunday dinner was over, spend the afternoon there and leave about eight o'clock, so that we could be home easily by nine. Of course, Jim was left behind to guard the place, but that dog worried and if we were at all late he would come to look for us. If we were not back by 8.45, he would set off along the lanes, through the intervening two villages, until he met the car coming from the opposite direction. Jim knew the sound of the car, and always stopped to wait by the roadside until we were abreast of him when we'd open the door, in he would jump and ride home with us. We worked it out, from the time and point at which he met us, that Jim must have left the farm at 8.45, winter or summer. As for knowing which route we had taken, well, we had to put it down to animal intuition!

Because of his upbringing Dad was a confirmed teetotaller and non-smoker. The non-smoking part stemmed from a physical shortcoming rather than religious conviction, for, if he was in a smoky atmosphere – such as a whist-drive – for any length of time, he became violently ill. Still, it was very convincing when linked with the non-drinking part.

Now there was an odd twist to his teetotal condition: it concerned only bought liquor, and even then was only partially true. Fo example, my mother would buy a bottle of sherry for Christmas, and the adults at that time would consume one glassful during Christmas evening, and another on Boxing night. The bottle was then firmly corked and put away in the kitchen dresser cupboard. Unless we had bibulous visitors during the year (and then they'd have to ask specifically as my folks would never remember it), there it stayed until the following Christmas. One year it was Mother's proud boast that she'd made one bottle of sherry last three years!

The fact that Mother made gallons of very potent home-made wine which everyone drank didn't seem to register with Dad, he was still teetotal. His brother, our Uncle Sid, was tall, thin, pale of face, and he really did like a drop. In fact it was whispered in the family that he'd actually been seen in an inn on market day, drinking – of all things – whisky! Now my dad was of opposite build; stocky, thick-set and with a ruddy, country-fresh complexion. Imagine his chagrin when he overheard someone refer to him as the 'red-faced brother who drank'. There's no justice! All the good fruits of the countryside were used in my mother's wine making – gooseberries, plums, cowslips, brambles . . . apparently the bramble wine was famous in the locality, its badge of quality being that it clung to the side of the glass.

The favourite wine with us children was the elderberry. It was used exclusively in a medicinal capacity, for when we had coughs or colds we were given a cupful of hot elderberry just before going to bed. Whether this did the cold any good I do not know, but we normally sank into a soporific stupor and certainly had a good night's sleep. I can remember now that feeling of warm, lazy contentment just before going to sleep: often I tried to keep myself awake just to savour the sensation but to no avail – the elderberry was too powerful.  There was one winter when we had a succession of sore throats, colds and sniffles. The elderberry went down at an alarming rate until Frank unwisely thought he had been ousted from his place in the rota: Mother overheard him telling Ray that it wasn't fair – it was his turn to have a cold that night!

I loved those cold winter nights. We didn't have such things as hot-water bottles but a brick, heated in the side oven, then wrapped in an old bit of flannel was wonderfully comforting in bed. If we forgot to put the brick in early enough that was no problem: we just lifted out one of the solid oven shelves, wrapped it up in an old shirt and took that to bed. The disadvantage came of course when they'd cooled off during the night; the flannel had slipped a bit, and when you turned over you stubbed your toe on a cold brick!

One evening, Dad harnessed Tommy to the milk-float and went to see Coddy to discuss next year's quantity, prices and arrangements for the milk. This always took place at the end of December, and on this New year's Eve Dad duly went after the evening's milking and said he'd be back by ten o'clock. It was a dark night with flurries of snow in the air and a keen wind whipping down from the Wolds and the sea.

At eleven o'clock, we began to worry as the weather had worsened, the snow falling heavily and drifting in the rising wind. At midnight Mother ignored the passing of the old and the coming of the new; she was utterly convinced that Dad was dead in a snowdrift: we had all got up of course to help her worry. There we were, standing shivering by the open kitchen door, the lamplight reflecting eerily from the swirling snow and wondering what on earth to do, when through the howls of the wind we thought we heard singing. We did: not accurate in either pitch or key, but the words of *All Things Bright and Beautiful* came clearly and familiarly to us: we stood in shocked disbelief. In a break of the storm, we discerned Tommy trot down the lane and into the stackyard. A few minutes later Dad staggered to the door, ' . . . the Lord God made them all'.

Mother was livid and in a voice to match the weather wanted to know where the ***** he'd been, and added for good measure: 'You're drunk, man!'

'Oh no, I'm not', retorted Dad, 'you know I'm teetotal. Coddy and I have only been having a sip or two of his wheat wine!'

In the ensuing furore, Tommy was completely forgotten and no one thought to feed him and bed him down. However, never a pony to bear a grudge – he knew he'd earned his keep by bringing the Master back without benefit of rein – so he ambled into the stackyard and helped himself at the haystack, managing to pull out and collapse a good half of the stack. In the morning, still harnessed to the milk-float, there was Tommy waiting to take the morning's milk down to Coddy. Yet another occasion on

which he had the last laugh, as I reckon Dad's head thumped every time Tommy put his elegant little feet on the road, despite the covering of snow.

My dad loved all his animals dearly. His horses he cosseted, brushed, combed, fed, watered and mucked out, all to an accompaniment of soothing conversation, gentle admonitions and terse instructions to 'move ovver' so that he could clean the other side. They would nuzzle and snuffle at him and he'd tell them to 'Give ovver, do, don't be so daft!'

With his calves he had a more maternal relationship. When they were taken from their mothers so soon after birth he obviously felt they needed a special friend in the great, wide world. He was prepared to be that friend. He fed them out of buckets with separated milk – sticking his fingers into their mouths to make them suck up the milk and so teaching them to drink. He talked to them like a Dutch Uncle, he rubbed their backs, pulled their ears and tickled their tummies – and they loved him and thought that they too were human. Any spare moment would find him sitting astride one of the doors to the calf boxes, discussing the state of the world with them, the price of wheat, and how lazy his brother-in-law was: all this at great length. The calves snuffled and nodded wisely as Dad made his points and clarified his ideas – odd, as in human company he couldn't make a speech to save his life!

The lambs were a different matter again. They all seemed to come into the world during the cold, wet and windy nights of winter. Dad would sit up in an old Windsor chair by the stoked up kitchen range, feet in hob-nailed boots stretched comfortably on the oldest snip-rug Mother could lay her hands on. Every hour, on the hour, Dad would wake up, put on his coat and go out into the yard where

the sheep were penned up between the straw sheaves and help
any sheep in difficulties. He would rub down the wet, new-born
lambs with wisps of hay; return the lambs to their mothers to be
licked and invited to suckle. Any lamb which had the misfortune
to lose its dam would be brought into the kitchen for the rest of
the night and put to dry on an old sack. In the morning, the
orphans would be put together in a box cosily filled with straw,
and then the trial of bottle-feeding began. (Sheep who had lost
their own lambs were very loth to adopt motherless ones – they
didn't smell right!) Warm cow's milk was the order of the day
and it soon became my job to administer this at weekends as it

was so time-consuming. Once the lambs were fed by human hand they formed quite close relationships with whoever was responsible for them.

How my dad always managed to wake up at exactly the same time I don't know: neither did he! He kept this facility for being able to wake just whenever he wanted, right into old age. If, for example, I needed to be awake at 5.30 a.m. to catch an early train back to college, sure enough at 5.25 a.m. precisely Dad would knock on my door. He was as accurate as any modern alarm clock, and much more pleasant about it.

Dad and birds did not relate to each other. After all, who could hold a conversation with an old hen except to swear at it in exasperation when it refused to enter its hut at night. I never saw my dad asking a hen or duck for its opinion on the price of corn, or whether to try to sell more turkeys on the Christmas market! But with calves it was a different matter; they would look him in the eye and tell him to hang on to the corn for another week or two as the price was sure to go up. They could also tell him it was a waste of his time going to church – he'd be far better employed walking down the Levels to see if the barley was looking fine.

Tommy was, of course, in yet another category. He ranged from: 'Good owd lad' to 'that perishing beast', according to his latest behaviour! After one particularly trying morning when he felt very frisky and refused to be cajoled into his harness for at least half an hour I even heard him called: 'That damned animal!' That was the nearest I ever heard my dad come to swearing. Tommy never took Dad seriously: he laughed at him, teased him, played with him but always . . . in the end . . . did a sound job of work. Life was, in Tommy's opinion, there to be enjoyed, and it was certainly not going to be his fault if he didn't enjoy it!

As the different seasons came round fruit was collected from the garden and bottled. We had no jars with modern tops, no rubber rings and snap closures, not even greaseproof paper – Mother relied on the old-fashioned mutton fat. This had the merit of being cheap (in fact, the butcher often gave it away), and with the additional benefit that it could be rendered down and used again the following year. We always used the large size of jam jar and these we filled with plums, gooseberries, blackcurrants, or whatever was in plentiful supply from the garden. The filled jars were put into the side oven for the fruit to cook slowly, then taken out and the juice topped up with boiling water. Hot, melted mutton fat was then poured into the neck of the jar. Of course the fat rose quickly to the surface and as the water cooled the fat set hard and formed a complete seal. Cheap and easy. There was only one snag: mice. They liked the taste of the fat and the jars had to be monitored constantly. It was difficult to keep the mice at bay especially in the autumn when they would come in from the fields in search of easier pickings. Our brigade of cats, lead by the redoubtable Stump, was the first line of defence.

Pig-killing was another busy time and everyone, even the men and boys, had to help. We always had a large fat pig, the fatter the better as this was rendered down and the resulting lard stored in large crocks for pastry-making. We cleaned the intestines and used the skin for the sausages; pork pies and brawns were made by the dozen; and for Christmas we made mincemeat, with real meat in it, not just suet; every last little bit of the pig was utilised in some way or other. It usually took two whole days of hard work. On the second day the pig's fries were arranged on plates and usually I had the job, when older, of leaving a fry at every cottage in the village. This was common practice; we knew we'd have a fry in return whenever other pigs were killed. The plates were always returned, unwashed, with a halfpenny on them for good luck.

Pork pies were made the following day and cooked in batches of six at a time in the old bread oven – the only time in the year when this oven was used. The story was that somehow this oven gave a better flavour to the pies; they were highly glazed with beaten egg and looked very impressive. As they were cooling off Mother made a hole in the top of each pie, placed a paper funnel in the hole and poured in the jelly. Traditionally, pies were given to friends and relatives from far and near: we loved them to start with but enthusiasm waned long before we had reached the last. Sausages kept better and so there was not the rush to have to eat them. Why they didn't go 'off' I don't know: they'd hang from the beams in the big dairy – one would just go in and cut off as many links as were necessary for the next meal. Of course in the middle of winter the dairy was like an ice-house, but I must admit that the last of the sausages had that furry look about them. I suppose Mother just cooked them a little longer as none of us seemed to come to grief. Once the more immediate tasks were finished, the large bacon joints and the hams were put in the brine troughs, the salt and saltpetre rubbed in and the curing process had begun.

I wonder what would have been the reaction of my family to the modern deep freezer and its contents in the supermarkets of today!

Like all country people in the 20s and 30s, we seemed to be nearly self-sufficient in looking after our own health. Elderberry wine was the specific used for colds and sore throats, the only addition to that was the tying of a sock – just removed from the foot – round one's throat just before going to bed. Any cuts and bruises were dealt with by a lavish application of iodine, and if a cut had the bad taste to go septic then all that was required was a bread poultice or two – a certain cure.

What we dreaded most was a tooth-ache: that was not so easily dealt with. Our milk teeth were straightforward as we were so keen to get the fairy money from under our pillows that we pushed and wobbled them so they parted company quite easily. If by any chance, one did prove stubborn then a piece of button thread was tied round the offending tooth while the other end was fastened to a small brass door-knob. Dad would then distract us by asking us to nod when we were ready and slamming the door before we had time to answer! It always worked: when we opened our eyes there would be the little white tooth, dangling on the end of the string.

Our adult teeth didn't always prove so easy to dislodge, so more archaic measures were resorted to—the vinegar plaster! A square of brown paper had vinegar poured onto it, then it was well-peppered, folded, and placed on the jaw above the offending tooth. The plaster was held in place by a scarf tied round the head: the agony from the peppered paper always made us forget, temporarily at least, the agony from the tooth. On one occasion,

Dad – to hurry things up – held a warm iron to the plaster quite convinced that this would do the trick. After all, he averred, when Mum had back-ache he put brown paper there and ironed that! After one particularly steamy session, Mum finally persuaded Dad that the services of a dentist really were needed. That was the break-through. The next time I had persistent tooth-ache I was taken to the town to see the dentist. This was an experience for which I was

totally unprepared: so was the dentist. I bit him so hard that he bled profusely. I was removed in disgrace and told to come back later when my nerves were stronger. That would give his nerves time to recover also!

Of course, we had no running water, no gas nor electricity. Everything was

done the hard way; even the simple action of using the lavatory was made more difficult. We had a two-hole (one large, one infant-size) convenience standing in its own spacious grounds – right at the bottom of our long garden. The sheer agony of finding you needed to visit the shack on a cold winter's night when it was raining and blowing had to be felt to be believed. I always suspected that the boys took a short cut; they never seemed to take as long as Mum or I.

Saturday night was bath-night. This was quite a performance: the boiler filled to brimming, kitchen fire stoked up, the clothes-horse with towels brought in – then the tin bath manhandled in from the wash-house! The bung was tested to see that it was firmly in position, and in went the water: then, hey-presto, we were scrubbed! I mean that, literally. Mother really did believe that cleanliness was next to Godliness and she laid on properly. Every so often, the bath was topped up with another ladle full of hot water. This bath routine was always carried out strictly according to age and therefore as I was in bed first I never found out whether Mum and Dad scrubbed one another pink as well.

Mother reserved mid-afternoons for her ablutions at the kitchen sink. It was a reasonably safe time, for all the men would be well away working in the fields. She could bank on being undisturbed, but as a safeguard I was always posted outside the kitchen window as an early warning system. One afternoon I was so engrossed watching my mother stark-naked, washing herself all over that I did not hear the farmer from down the lane approaching. He joined me at the window to see what I had found so fascinating. I was most unpopular; the farmer was delighted; Mother was not amused.

4.

OF CHICKENS, DUCKS, AND WANDERING COWS

AS SOON AS WE WERE OLD ENOUGH, we were all given regular jobs to do about the farm – such as shutting up the poultry houses every night. This was a time-consuming task as we had chickens all over the place: four huts in the Home Field, two in the Pingles and four more down the Levels. Now chickens are contrary birds; for one thing they will not roost until it is nearly dark, and there are always one or two still outside, pecking away for the last little morsel. Therefore, in summer time, it could be nearly ten o'clock before they were ready and if you arrived a little early no amount of driving or shoo-ing would get them in. The recalcitrant ones would cackle in dismay, and dart away to be joined by those already in the hut. They'd all come tumbling out to see what the fuss was about, then they'd join in the fun. Many a time I sat on the fence waiting for the last hen to make up its mind: even if I was tired and hungry, they did not seem to be.

Ducks were a much easier proposition. All one had to do was call them: after a few moments they would come plodding, one after another in single file, from all directions. They would patiently line up to enter giving quiet, contented quacks as they waddled along, telling each other of the super day they'd had, all the tasty bits they'd managed to unearth and the lovely swim they'd had in the beck. Occasionally of course, they'd be scathing about the unwelcome attentions they'd had to suffer from one of the drakes!

Frank and I had to do the hen rounds in turn, brother Ray being elevated to higher duties. His lot in life was to help wash down after the evening's milking; not a pleasant job as it could be pretty vile after the cows had been waiting in turn to be milked. Ray vowed that they all waited to relieve themselves (my words, not his!) until they came into the shed. As all the water had to be pumped by hand into buckets and then thrown down the stone floor to aid the brushing away of all the mess, it was quite hard work for a ten-year-old lad. Dad was very particular about cleanliness, so finally the whole place had to be swilled down with clear water. In summer this was not too bad a job, but in the depths of winter it was wet and bitterly cold labour.

My weekend task was to wash the chicken and duck eggs. This was done standing at the sandstone kitchen sink and water from the side boiler of the kitchen range was ladled into a tin bowl over the eggs. When all the straw, dirt and feathers were removed, they'd be rinsed in another bowl, then dried, counted and packed into boxes. As we had to eat all the cracked eggs ourselves, and as I didn't really like eggs all that much, it was an exercise that taught me care and concentration. One of the better jobs was hunting for broody hens who were 'laying-away', that is, hiding their nests in the long grass hoping to escape detection, and hatch off their own eggs. We normally managed to find them: we'd lie in wait until they thought they were unobserved when they'd sneak off into the nettles or the granary or the chaff-house where it was warm and quiet. Sometimes, however, a Rhode Island Red would appear, prating proudly, leading a line of yellow balls of fluff, as much as to say, 'Who's the clever one now?'

My favourite job was tenting the cows. This meant looking after the cows, ensuring they did not stray and supervising them. A railway line ran through part of the farm and we had two sets of crossing gates to negotiate with horses and carts, and later, tractors. These gates were a great nuisance in harvest time because of the frequent day-trip trains going to the coast resort in the morning and returning in the evenings. But at cow-tenting time, these gates came into their own!

The job involved taking the cows from the Home Field, where in late summer the grass had become short, especially if the weather had been hot and dry, and driving them to eat off the lusher grass on the sides of the local lanes. I used to arm myself with a book, an apple or two and any food that I could sneak out of the dairy, and set off with the cows. First preference was the lane leading up to the crossing gates; with reasonable luck they'd be closed against road traffic and so the cows couldn't wander too far. I would establish myself at the entrance to the lane about two hundred yards from the first set of gates, find a shady spot and settle down with my book. This was comparative bliss: bees would work from plant to plant; larks, high in the sky would trill away in the sheer joy of existence, and it always seemed to be high summer. This was the life!

Just occasionally, things went wrong. One day I recall quite clearly: the book was a Sherlock Holmes story and I was totally immersed. I did not notice that the gates had been opened to let a horse and waggon from a neighbouring farm through until the clopping of the iron-clad feet brought me back to the world of reality. I shot to my feet to see half my charges enjoying the chance to reach the other side. I'm sure the grass was no greener there, but cows – being such curious creatures – just had to find out for themselves. Angrily I ran down to fetch them back, the rest of the herd rousing their somnolent heads to ascertain the cause of this haste on such a lazy summer evening. Reaching the furthest cow, I gave a short version of my opinion and turned them back. However, the crossing keeper, a Mr Bell who enjoyed his little joke, had meanwhile closed the gates and successfully cut my charges into two small herds. Only after much pleading, wheedling and cajoling did he deign to re-open the gates and allow us back. I suppose the rest of the herd wanted to know if it had been worth all the trouble, but I was in no mood of whimsy – I discovered my abandoned apple and cake were black with ants!

My Mum was, within the limits of her kitchen facilities, a very good cook. She made excellent fruit cakes and her apple pasties were delicious. All the cooking was done in the side oven of the kitchen range; it was an art to keep the fire at an even temperature, wood and coal had to be kept at the ready to be put in the fire when needed.

There was, of course, no running water; all had to be pumped up by hand from the big pump at the side of the old

sandstone sink. The drain from this sink boasted no U-bend but went straight out to the drain beneath the window. The top of the opening was covered by a small brass plate pierced with holes. When the wind blew from the north it caused this brass plate to jump and clatter in its bed, a noise which one couldn't ignore.

It was a great day when the Primus stove was bought and installed at the side of the sink, the range of Mother's cooking was greatly extended as, before, everything had to be either boiled or steamed over the kitchen fire; now she could be more versatile! Another side benefit was that in summer we did not always need a fire in the kitchen, a bonus when the temperature was in the eighties.

During one of our more affluent periods we had a girl from the village, Martha, a daughter of the waggoner from the next farm, come to assist with the housework. This was a great help as Mother did a lot of the yardwork and feeding calves when the men were busy in the fields. Martha was going to marry a labourer from the next village so wanted to work for a few months near home until she was wed. Mother tried very hard to improve Martha's cooking, with little success; instead of being a natural at it, she was  decidedly unnatural. She stayed on to help after her marriage and absolutely convulsed Mother when she described her attempts to make her husband a rice pudding for his Sunday dinner. Apparently it was so hard and stuck to the dish with such firmness that she had to slip out into the garden and bury the lot, dish as well!

We always seemed to have friends and relatives staying with us, especially during the school holidays. One Easter we had an uncle, aunt, and two cousins from London staying for two whole weeks. On the middle Sunday Mum decided to push the boat out and really give them a treat, so she asked my Dad to get her a brace of pheasants, which was something they would never have in their own home! Now this request was rather difficult to comply with as none of the tenant farmers held their own shooting rights which were retained by the land owners. The only things we were allowed to have were pigeons, rabbits, or hares as these could damage the crops if not kept within bounds. Consequently now and again Dad was reduced to doing a bit of mild poaching on his own farm and shooting the odd pheasant and partridge late at night or early in the morning when no one was about. He wasn't very keen to do this but when he looked out of the bedroom in the early dawn and saw three or four pheasants parading on his lawn beneath the window, it was difficult to resist the temptation to nip downstairs, get his twelve bore shotgun, creep upstairs again and pot a couple through the window – anyway Mum did so enjoy a bit of pheasant. When he did this, of course, he frightened all the others who were fast asleep, nearly into Kingdom Come!

Eventually he consented to try on this occasion, after all it was about three months since the last bit of poaching. A couple of days later he proudly brought in a brace of beauties – so Mother took them into the Boiling House and proceeded to pluck them. A few minutes later Sally, the small daughter of Ted Bush, one of our labourers, poked her little head round the door and watched the goings-on with great interest. Eventually overcoming her shyness she looked at Mum and said, 'Yuv got a pretty bod – me da gits uz one ivry week!' Mother was amazed, and furious to think that she'd had to wheedle to get a couple now and again and the workforce were poaching on a regular basis and living off the fat of the land. I think she was even more cross to realize Dad couldn't say anything to Bushy because he himself was in an untenable position! Anyway, the birds were duly cooked, with all the trimmings, and much appreciated by the town folk.

About once every five years Mother would manage to have a few days holiday with her sister and brother. Dad, living near his parents and brother and sister, did not realise how sometimes she longed to see her family. One spring Mother decided she really would have to have a short break and see them, so leaving Dad and the boys to the not so tender mercies of his, as yet unmarried, sister, she took me with her to stay with her elder brother and his family in London. He was one of the marvellous Bobbies attached to the House of Commons who, as a matter of pride, knew every Member by name. He was a tall, very well-built man in his late forties – and the possessor of a booming, sonorous voice. This frightened me to death! In the living room my aunt had a round dining table always covered in a red velvet cloth. This hung down until it nearly touched the floor and apparently as soon as I heard my uncle's step outside the door I took refuge under this table and no amount of bribery or cajolery would entice me to come out. Mother swears I stayed under that table at the weekend for two whole days, only coming out to go to bed – then only when Uncle conveniently left the room! How shy can you get?

On one never to be forgotten day Mother, Aunt, and I went into the city to see the sights and came across a crowd of people on Putney Bridge. We joined the crowd and leant over the bridge to look at the river and see what was causing the interest. Presently two boats came shooting along and we realised we had a grandstand view of the Oxford and Cambridge Boat Race – not that it meant much to a five year old!

I have mentioned the railway line that passed through our fields, and the gatehouse and crossing. Mr Bell, the crossing keeper, left the gates open for the trains all the time and just reversed them when the farm vehicles actually arrived at the gates. One very hot summer's day he decided as all the nearby farms were bringing carts and wagons with loads of corn fairly frequently he would leave the gates open for the road and alter them when the trains were signalled into his section. He seated himself outside by his garden gate in readiness to do his work but whether the hot sun sent him to sleep we don't know. Obviously he suddenly realised a train was nearly on his gates by the train's whistle as he dashed up and tried to open his gates. He was much too late and the train crashed through them, killing him in the process. We all grieved for him and his elderly wife – so sad, so unnecessary.

While the village was still reeling from that shock, a small-holder whose land adjoined ours failed to turn up to help with the harvesting as he normally did – a lot of lease-lend help was practised in those days. When my dad called round to ask him if he could help the next day his wife said he's come if he could, but he wasn't feeling too well. He died two days later of infantile paralysis, which we later called Polio. This cast a blight on the whole village – why he should contract that when no-one else did, we couldn't understand. Anyway, life does go on and gradually other events do take precedence in the mind.

5.

In Which My Dad Suffers Promotion to Admiral

DOWN THE LEVELS was the most interesting part of the farm – in that the original village of the Middle Ages was situated about two hundred yards along the path. This was a public right of way.

Apparently when my parents first tenanted the farm there were many ruins of cottages. The stones from these were all removed to improve the crewyards. The village pond was still there however, also several fruit trees, obviously part of the old cottage gardens. Now one of these trees was a greengage! If my mother had one weakness it was that she loved a good, ripe greengage above any other fruit. Therefore they were inspected daily until they were judged to be just right. On the day in question, a beautiful, mellow, golden summer afternoon, my brother Frank was deputised to take a fairly light ladder and two milk cans and pick the greengages. Half an hour later he came back with one full can which he deposited on the kitchen table. When Mother pointed out that she thought there should be more he agreed but said it was impossible to reach them as they were in an awkward position to get at.

'Well', said my mother, 'that's all right, your sister can help you, she'll hold the ladder'. So off we went and came to the tree in question. I could see the problem, the branches were thin, brittle and old, and certainly couldn't take the weight of the ladder and my brother. Then Frank had the brilliant idea that I should go underneath the ladder and as he mounted it I should push against his weight. Surprisingly this seemed to work. He gingerly mounted and when high enough he carefully began picking the greengages and cautiously placing them in the can. So far, so good. Pleased with the success I began to look around at the lovely sky; bunches of plums; the lovely leaves on the bushes at my side, when suddenly, in the long, damp grass around the base of a berberis (another relic from a cottage

garden) I found myself meeting two black, beady, unwinking eyes. A duck was sitting there enjoying an afternoon siesta in the shade.

Now anyone who knows me even to this day will tell you I'm absolutely besotted with ducks. I love them! I watch them, I fondle them, and talk to them in quacks. I think I must have been a duck in a previous incarnation. Therefore, quite without thinking, I let go of the ladder and went to have a chat with my blood brother. Suddenly there was a horrified yell from Frank, aloft in the tree, as the ladder began to move. I looked up in sheer disbelief as the ladder began to keel over; oh, so slowly, it seemed to take an age to reach the point of no return. I was too mesmerised to try to grab it.

Frank, very slowly and gracefully, performed the most perfect somersault, still clutching the can, straight into the pond. Unfortunately, many generations of ducks had used this pond for their ablutions, and other things, so that when Frank eventually struggled to his feet he was a sight to behold – black slime from head to foot! But, covered as his face was, it didn't hide his expression, a genuine desire for revenge! I straightaway assessed the situation as being fraught with danger for me and took to my heels – down the lane, over the gate and through the weakest part of the hedge round the kitchen garden. Straight across that, the sound of pursuit getting nearer, across the

causey I went, though the kitchen door, and shot the bolt just in time!

Having found momentary sanctuary I looked around to find more permanent safety. When I realised Mother was in the big dairy churning, I assumed a most innocent expression and wandered in to find out how she was getting on. But brother Frank was not so easily thwarted. Unable to batter the kitchen door down he went round to the back of the house, prised open the door to the coal cellar and came up into the big dairy from the other end.

'You little devil, I'll kill you for that,' he said, and made a grab for me. I dodged behind Mother just in time and so she caught the full force of his slimy blackness – all over her spotless, hygenic butter-making apron – to say nothing of the mess on the floor. She was furious and ordered him out the same way as he came! I then made my second mistake of the day, I laughed! Quick as a flash, Mother, all five feet ten, and well-made, turned and gave me a box on the ear, knowing full well, she said, that I must have earned it.

Frank was ordered to strip off every stitch of clothing in the back yard and wash in a bucket of warm water which she handed out to him. When dressed in clean clothes he was told to give his wet clothes a good rinse under the pump before putting them in the wash house. As I sat next to him at mealtimes my ankles were black and blue for a few days, I daren't retaliate as it would have been my luck to have caught either Mother or Father who sat at the end of the table. Two or three days later I slipped him my sweets which I'd saved from the weekend – (we had two on Saturday, and two on Sunday) so sweetness and light reigned until the next time. I did enjoy the expression on my brother's face when replying to Mother's query about the whereabouts of the remaining greengages! Both the can and plums were at the bottom of the pond. My other brother and I were sent, with a clothes prop, from the drying ground, to fish for the can. We eventually poked it out and washed it. It still had two plums in it!

Sometimes when lambs were born their mothers died and we had to take over as mother. We would bring them into the kitchen and put them into a flannel lined box if they were very weak, although it was always better of course to leave them in the loose-boxes to be fed all together. The very weak had to be cossetted though – and one year we really had to fight to save one little fellow, feeding him warm cow's milk, well watered, every hour or so. We christened him Larry, after the Children's Hour character, and after a day or two he decided life was worth living. However the weather was very wet, cold and stormy, and being soft-hearted we kept him in the kitchen for a few more days. That was a mistake – when we put Larry into the loose-box in the buildings with the three other orphans he refused to mix with them, sleeping on his own in the corner. When they were released into the field as the weather improved he was still a loner! He spent hours at the field gate near the house baa-ing plaintively for attention. Everytime the gate was left open he darted through – straight up the yard and into the kitchen where he settled down by the fire. He was quite convinced he was a human being! When we crossed the field to board the school bus he walked all the way with us and as soon as we appeared in the afternoon he dashed along and walked home with us.

Eventually Dad gave up the unequal struggle and Larry had the run of the stockyard and came to the kitchen door whenever he felt like it. I noticed Dad sent him to the market with the first of the fat lambs – the boys and I were most upset but there's no place for sentiment in farming.

One year we had a larger litter of pigs than usual, Dad thought he'd done very well. However as time went on we noticed one of the piglets was not as large as the others, he was the runt of the litter! No amount of extra rations would induce him to put on weight to catch up with the others. We christened him Oswald after Mosley. The time came for the rest of the litter to go to market but not even the most optimistic could have supposed anyone would be so blind as to buy Oswald, in fact he would spoil the chance of a good price for the rest of the piglets. So Dad uttered the dreaded words, 'It's no good, we'll have to kill him and eat him ourselves'. Never has pig-killing day been greeted with less enthusiasm. To cut a long story short he was duly slaughtered, salted and dried! Mother half-heartedly cut some of the bacon into a boiling-sized joint, cooked it and brought it to the table. It was disgusting! So hard that one could barely cut it, and the taste! Even Dad said the dogs could have it. Not even the hams were much good.

Like all farmer's wives my mother looked after the hens and ducks and also made butter. The proceeds from these kept the house going, providing us all with food and clothes. Therefore when the egg yield dropped it was a matter of concern. After investigation it was decided that some of the hens, not wanting to avail themselves of the incubator for hatching their eggs, decided to strike a blow for independence and hatch their own; in fact they were 'laying-away'.

I was therefore deputed to lie in wait and see if I could pin-point where they were going to ground, in the stables, cow house or somewhere among the buildings. After a time I saw one or two sneaking off into the orchard which did happen to be waist high in nettles. I sneaked along to the side and found an old abandoned hay-rake which I climbed in order to have a better view. Unfortunately I put my weight too far back on the seat and what was left of the shafts shot up in the air and I performed a gentle nose-dive into those nettles. I screamed in pain and fright and beat my way out to the side – hens flying in all directions. I'd certainly found their secret hideaway, tho' at no small cost to myself! Mother came dashing to the rescue, frantically pulling up dock leaves to place on the afflicted parts. Everyone knows that dock leaves don't work unless you spit on them before covering the rash. I was in agony and Mum soon ran out of spit. I had to sleep on top of the bed that night – I daren't get warm. I left someone else to raid the hen's nests.

One hot summer's day Ray and I were running round chasing Jim the dog in the Home Field. We soon tired of this as it was too hot so we wandered over to the big pond. This is usually full of ducks dibbling for juicy particles in the water or merely floating lazily, heads tucked over on to their backs, eyes closed, fast asleep. The cows also made this spot their own, standing up to their knees in the socky water, tails aswishing to keep the flies away, anything to get cool in this sultry hot weather. But today was different because the pond was totally dried up – the clay bottom was criss-crossed with deep fissures like crazy paving where the loss of moisture had made it contract. So of course we climbed down to this virgin territory to investigate. There were no treasures to be found on this pond bottom but Ray spotted something of great interest in the pond bank – a hole leading to a wasps' nest. We watched in silence as these busy little creatures flew in and out, full of their own importance. Now Ray did happen to be swinging a stick in his hand and it was the work of a moment to poke it into the wasps' hole and give it a few hearty twists and turns, then like the heroic figure he was, he turned and ran! If I'd had my wits about me of course I'd have done the same – needless to say I didn't, I stood and watched, goggle-eyed and mouth agape as these, by now thoroughly angry wasps flew out in large squadrons to defend their home against all comers! I was obviously the aggressor and also a sitting, or to be more exact, a standing target. With swept back wings, stings at the ready, grins of anticipation on their faces, they homed in on me.

Too late I realised my danger, but having been stung twice the spirit of cowardice (or self preservation) took over and I fled for the field gate, over the yard wall and into the kitchen, hotly pursued by the odd lone fighter! I think I cleared the wall with inches to spare and I'd never even managed to jump it before. Sheer terror can be a powerful spur. Mother came to the rescue once again, with the blue bag from the wash-house this time. Not that it seemed to do much good – I had five stings in various places and was in agony for at least two days. Brother Ray did look a little shame-faced about it but that didn't make the swelling go down! I gave the pond a very wide berth for weeks afterwards in case wasps are blessed with memories.

One year we had a very wet summer, it rained and rained – eventually the ground became water-logged. At first my Dad was pleased to see the water as he said the growing crops needed it but, as must be expected in the farming world, it didn't know when to stop! Some of the fields were practically under water and that was ruining the crops, so he said.

One morning, after a particularly wet night we discovered that the road to 'The Levels' was under water. This lane was about one hundred yards long, a sunken way between two fairly high hedges. What with the dyke alongside the lane, the beck on the other side of the southern field and the old village pond at the end of the lane, flooding was not to be wondered at, as both pond and beck had overflowed to the surrounding ground. Dad duly slopped his way along the lane with the two buckets of chicken mash, fed the hens, collected the eggs and came home, congratulating himself that the chicken huts were on the higher ground beyond the pond.

The next day the rain continued and conditions deteriorated. When the lane to The Levels was inspected the water was found to have risen to an alarming height, in fact only the top of the five-barred gate was visible above the water! Now my dad is not the sort of person to be put off by such trifles – after giving the situation much thought he had what could only be termed as a brainwave. 'The bath! That's the thing', he said, 'I'll row down the lane to feed the chickens, there's nothing to it'. By now the whole family was standing around in one of the brief periods of weak sunshine, all giving our opinions— unsolicited of course.

So the bath which we used every Saturday night was now to be launched upon the flood waters it seemed. Mother raised a few half-hearted objections, more from the point of view of damaging the bath than Dad's safety. Of course we children were all in favour and gave the escapade our unqualified approval.

So the bath was fetched and floated, Dad first making sure the bung in the bottom was fully knocked home. He then fetched the two buckets of chicken mash, waded out in his wellies and placed them carefully in the bath, the bottom rim of one bucket over the bung so that he didn't knock it out when he boarded his vessel. Providing himself with a spade so that he could paddle his punt he stepped into the bath. Unfortunately his weight was considerably more than the combined weight of the two buckets so that the bath tipped alarmingly to one end, causing the cargo to shoot to the other end. Eventually he found that by kneeling in the middle he was more or less master of his craft. So off he set. As our bath was rounded at both ends it didn't really matter which way it was facing so steering was a matter of by guess or by God; sometimes it went in circles, other times it shyly nosed itself into the hedge only to be given a hearty shove off with the spade.

We all stood on fairly dry land and shouted encouragement to the intrepid mariner but eventually when Dad was half way on his somewhat erratic course down the lane where the water was at its deepest, we were suddenly conscious that all was not as it

should be. For some mysterious reason Dad suddenly seemed a lot lower in the water and the more frantically he paddled the lower he got. In desperation he made to stand up, over-balanced and disappeared over the side.

By this time Owd Sam had left his work in the yard and come to see what all the noise was about. I shall never forget the sight of his face, which was brown, weathered and really lived-in, with tears of laughter finding their way down the seams in his old cheeks. The sight of 'The Maister' floundering up to his armpits in water, fighting his way, with water laden wellies back to us, delighted his old soul.

Tommy, the New Forest pony, was an interested observer to all these goings-on. He was in the field to the north of the lane which was considerably higher than the rest and so was comparatively dry. He watched Dad's antics with great interest; this was something new, not recorded in the folk memory of the New Forest pony! He trotted along on his elevated side walk, neighing encouragement at this entertaining sight. When Dad finally sank from view Tommy peered anxiously over his hedge until he rose again – then I'll swear that animal was laughing. Not so Jimmy the dog. He was going frantic, barking until finally his fear for his master overcame his acute dislike of water and he dashed in at full paddle to escort Dad to safety, grinning with delight as he finally shepherded him out of the water. Dad was a sorry sight. His comments were such as no carefully brought up Methodist would surely have uttered.

The cause of the disaster was deemed to be his initial boarding of the bath, when the buckets slid down to the other end. They'd loosened the bung and the water had filtered in under the cargo, until the bung came out altogether.

As the chickens still needed feeding Owd Sam offered to do it. 'How?' was Dad's ungraciously angry response. 'Weele – Maister', said Owd Sam, 'if'n Oi tak t'mash along o yon cloase an cress that'n cloase oi'll be jest roit for t'be at back'n yon 'uts wi 'ens is!'

Of course he was right, if Dad had gone along the lane the other way, crossed Tommy's field and then the next one, he'd have been directly behind the chicken huts in the next field.

Owd Sam stumped off to mix more mash, he was still crying with laughter and shaking his head at the same time; not often he got topside of the Maister. Jimmy anxiously escorted his God up to the kitchen door and on this occasion he went into the kitchen just to be sure he was quite safe. Only then did he leave him and go back to stare sadly at the scene of the disaster.

We children of course thought the whole episode highly funny and, for days afterwards, when Dad was near enough to hear we'd enquire of one another the whereabouts of the 'Admiral' and whether it was good sailing weather today! In the end he said he'd take a rope's end to us and we'd have to walk the plank. A couple of days later when the water had subsided Mother rescued the buckets and the bath. The bath was brought up to the yard and disinfected. She then fetched out the paint left over from the last time the kitchen was painted, so the bath became Lincoln Green on the outside and 'drab-stone' on the inside. 'That won't show the tidemarks!' she said, with satisfaction and unconscious humour.

Our house was very old, parts of it dating back to the time of the first Elizabeth; other parts had been added at different times but it all blended together to make home. It was a friendly house though I sometimes thought it had a mind of its own. It certainly had its likes and dislikes.

It liked many people living in it and seemed to expand to accommodate all the cousins, friends and relations who flocked there at holiday time, especially harvest time. Everyone went into the fields and worked hard until daylight faded, then as the twilight deepened we trudged home in the dusk, the horses' harness clinking and our muted voices the only comment on the day. As the men took the horses to the stables to rub down and feed, we children ambled towards the kitchen door, always wide open, the yellow lamplight spilling out across the yard.

We took it in turns to pump up the water at the kitchen sink to wash our grubby hands and plunge our dusty, sun-tanned faces into bowls of cold water. As we settled down to wait for the men to finish all their jobs my mother continued to put the finishing touches to the supper, stepping over legs stretched out in exhaustion, walking round people too lazy to move out of the way. It was cool after the heat of the day, the thick stone walls denying the power of the sun.

At last the men would come in, the buckets being clanked down on the yard as they made for the ever-open door. The house waited and welcomed them – eight or ten people making a move to sit at the scrub-topped kitchen table, my dad picking up his carving knife and fork and proceeding to slice cold bacon and cold beef for the hungry plates. The pickles and beetroot were passed round, the fried potatoes were ladled out and everyone settled to eat in contented silence – the occasional hand stretching out for the butter or another chunk of bread. Once the plates were empty it was the time for the apple pasties to appear, crisp pastry on the outside and luscious fruit on the inside. We all took a piece, the children hoping for the biggest portion as my mother's pasties were justly famed. Replete, we settled back for a chat and comment on the extent of the progress in the 'twenty-acre' or the prospects of continued fine weather for the next day. Those that had any energy left lethargically quit their seats and helped with the washing up.

As one or two heads began to droop my mother started to shoo us upstairs to our beds, or mattresses on the floor for the hefty boy cousins. We settled down quickly and were soon asleep, too tired to get up to any mischief. The house settled down around us, creaking and protesting a little as its ancient floors and walls resumed their accustomed positions; if the owls hooted in the near-by barn we did not hear them.

Our house disliked storms, especially those of the thunder variety: so did Mother! From my earliest days I can remember her, on hearing the first distant rumble of thunder, opening up all the doors so that it could come in and go out without let or hindrance – everything made of metal would be removed and hidden under a cloth so that it didn't attract the lightning. All these necessary chores done she collected me and we went and sat in the store-room under the stairs. This room was enclosed on all sides, there being no windows at all, just the one door. We then sat out the storm, the house clasping us safely to its bosom, keeping all danger at bay. As the thunder crashed around us the house shivered in protest, creaking, groaning and vibrating in time to the thumps of the thunder. One day there was an added crash to the cacophony, Mother and I looked at one another in terror, what had happened? The house hadn't let us down? When we eventually emerged we looked around to find what had caused the crash; everything appeared as normal, nothing out of place. It wasn't until my dad came home that we realised that the kitchen chimney had been struck by lightning and was lying at a somewhat drunken angle. No wonder the house didn't like storms.

One day in late summer Tommy decided he'd been good long enough – he needed another walkabout to relieve the boredom. He carefully let himself out of the paddock and ambled into the yard next to the farmhouse to see what was going on. To his delight, he discovered that the orchard was accessible from that side so in he ambled and helped himself to the fallen apples. Unfortunately he had picked a Monday morning for his ramble and so had to negotiate a billowing washing-line, but as any self-respecting pony would, he was careful to avoid the sheets flying in the blustery wind.

When my Dad emerged from the kitchen after his mid-morning snack, his yell could have been heard from afar; we all came dashing out to discover the cause of the uproar. Even Tommy cocked an enquiring eye to find out what the fuss was all about. He was soon left in no doubt as Dad advanced upon him. Retribution was at hand! Tommy's sense of self-preservation took over and he did a smart about-turn only to knock flying with his rump one of the clothes-props. The tension in the line released, the other prop slowly keeled over and the clothes line descended to within a few feet of the ground, doing the sheets no good at all. In an effort to escape the flapping white things Tommy charged forward breaking the line as he went – to emerge on the other side with a striped roller towel lying across his ample backside and a pair of Dad's long-legged pants draped coyly across his neck and over one ear. He took off at a smart trot down the lane to the village with Dad in hot pursuit, Ray yelling encouragement to Dad; Frank and I shouting support to Tommy.

Down the village street we streamed, the roller towel slipping off as Tommy broke into a canter. Dad yelled to the driver of an on-coming baker's cart to stop that . . . animal; he, poor man, a bemused expression on his face at the sight of a flying New Forest pony wearing underwear in an unaccustomed place, stood stock still with amazement!

Eventually Tommy, tiring of the chase, drew into a gateway and tried to shake the offending garment from his head. When Dad finally panted up alongside, he used such words to describe Tommy's behaviour that even Tommy was shocked.

We all trailed back to the orchard to assess the damage, only to find an irate Mother putting the sheets back into the copper to be re-washed. She was not amused but Tommy, from the glint in his eye, was having a great day.

6.

Village Characters

BIRTHS, MARRIAGES AND DEATHS were regarded as events of great interest, possibly because they were so few and far between in our sparse community. We had one wedding in eight years; funerals seemed to come a little more often however. When a birth occurred it was anticipated with relish by the whole community.

The local midwife, a railway-worker's wife who was completely untrained, was alerted to be on standby. She would arrive at the cottage with her bulging bag and take charge. Men were banished! Doctors were an unheard of luxury, only to be called in the direst emergency. All that the midwife seemed to do was to tie a roller towel to the brass rail at the head of the bed, tell the mother-to-be to 'Pull at the top end; push at the bottom end and yell if you want to, duck!' It always seemed to work.

One day, my dad and Owd Sam had their heads together, having a right old chortle over a juicy bit of gossip. Owd Sam said, 'Hai, maister, 'ave you 'eered as 'ow owd Bob Harris is back in't gander pen agen, poor owd sod?'

My mother's sympathies were with Mrs Harris – she already had six children!

The country districts always abounded in characters, possibly because in scattered communities they were more obvious. We of course, had our share. We always called the main road which joined our market town to the coast 'The Ramper', and it was noticed that at 4.00 p.m. most Thursdays a 'shag-an' or tramp always passed along the ramper, obviously on his way to the work-house where he would get supper, bed and breakfast before moving on. This man was always called 'Goff Thomson'. He was a great mystery to us all; there he would be, striding along, beard thrust forward, dressed in an old hat, grey macintosh tied with string around the middle, and carrying a little canvas bag on his back. If anyone passed the time of day with him he invariably answered politely in a most cultured voice. Someone in the nearby town once said that he'd come from a very good family and had obtained a degree at university.

One day a neighbour had to go on a business trip about 80 miles away and imagine his surprise when he saw Goff striding along the East Anglian roads. Had he changed his route after all this time? No, the following Thursday at 4.00 p.m. there he was, head down going for his bed for the night. What had happened to make him take to this way of life—was he the earliest drop-out?

Another person of interest was a young man who lived in the next village. He was a little simple – or, as I prefer, a 'natural' – but quite harmless; in fact we had a sneaking fondness for him. He had one great passion in life and that was going to church. Every Sunday he came to our village church in the morning, the next village in the afternoon, and evensong at his own church, so he walked miles. If there was a wedding or a funeral within distance that was a God-sent bonus. He always sat in the front pew and would gaze worshipfully at the parson. He sometimes had to be forcibly removed from the front pew at weddings as the bride's mother didn't always take kindly to being accompanied in her pew by Joe – and at funerals he was apt, if the verger was not on the alert, to turn up with the chief mourners. There wasn't an ounce of harm in him however, and we accepted him with no comment.

We had a very large church for the size of the village and the organ was a basic affair driven by a pumping mechanism. One Sunday we arrived for the morning service, sat down in our usual places, and the service began. We became aware during the first hymn that something was amiss; the organ, what we could hear of it, sounded definitely odd. On looking round we discovered that Walt, the organ blower, was absent from his post. He was normally very reliable, in fact we often wondered what hold the vicar had over him – probably gave him immunity from Sunday School! The organist, a widow from the next village was trying to cope by using the alternative pedals but it rather sounded as if the mice had feasted on the leather. She had her head down, bent forward and fingers pounding loudly on the keys whilst her legs were pumping like pistons. She looked as if she were in a stationary bicycle race trying to reach the gates of Heaven; all these efforts only produced a faint, complaining moan.

Mother gave brother Frank a nudge and nod, indicating that he was to go to the rescue. Frank was rather loth to do this as by this time the entire congregation was aware that something was amiss – the singing died away and we all turned to watch as poor Nellie pounded harder and harder, getting more and more red in the face – beads of perspiration were gathering on the end of her nose – this was much too good to stop – how long could she continue before disaster struck? Would she make it to the end of the hymn?

Suddenly it struck our friend Joe that all was not as it should be – so he left his pew and mounted the chancel steps so that he could see over the heads of the congregation. Not having sufficient height there he proceeded to climb into the pulpit where he diagnosed the source of the trouble. 'Gie yit mooer 'umpty, missus; Gie yit mooer 'umpty' he shouted. By now we were all convulsed with laughter – poor Nellie hadn't more 'umpty to give.

Mother decided enough was enough and dug brother Frank in the ribs so hard that he was catapulted into the aisle near the organ and obeyed her imperative finger. He grabbed the organ handle and proceeded to pump for dear life. Nellie, engrossed in her battle with feet and keys hadn't noticed him take over until she looked up suddenly and saw him, stopping promptly in mid-note in astonishment. All we heard was the clanking of the wooden handle, the organ shaking on its foundations and air escaping in all directions. Immediately sizing up the situation she bent to the task in hand again but Frank, seeing her stop playing, had stopped pumping so that all we heard now was the rattle of empty keys. After another false start they eventually got it together but by this time everyone was so bemused that we didn't know what verse we had reached so we sang different lines. Finally, Nellie called a halt to the proceedings by playing a definite 'Amen'.

In our village we had a labourer named Smith who, though a good worker at all the different farm tasks, was most unreliable. Sometimes he would work for one farmer, then another; he favoured about six or seven farms near the village. He would present himself in the yard and ask what was to be done and then carry on with the job for a few weeks or maybe only a few days then off he'd go and we'd hear he was working on another farm. As he didn't always wait for the weekend before he left he nearly always had a bit of money owing to him – but this was always religiously kept and given to him when next he appeared.

I well remember my Dad tearing him off a strip when he appeared one day – 'Why did you leave us in the middle of tatying? You're a blaming nuisance'. The old boy stood quietly and smiled until Dad had finished then he said: 'But where be oi to start t'day, Gaffer?' No amount of cajolery would make him stay anywhere long – no one knew whether it was just itchy feet, or could it be that every so often he'd just forget where he'd been the day before? It was a complete mystery to all the farmers but as he was a good workman it was accepted and he was always given a job. In villages you always looked after your own.

He had one other peculiarity. He obviously bought all his clothes from jumble sales but that couldn't possibly account for the fact that the seat of his trousers was always torn. Had he got a chair with a nail in an unfortunate place? Did he ease his way through barbed wire and so rip the seat of his trousers? No one knew, but one could usually see the tail of his striped flannel shirt shyly peeping through or even sometimes it would be poking out. One day he was gracing our farm with his presence, singling beet. Now it was common practice for some of the older boys to give themselves a few unofficial days holiday and to join in and earn a bit of money. This was encouraged by their parents and the schools turned a blind eye unless it became too blatant. On this particular day, there they were, singling beet, row by row in echelon when suddenly one of the lads looked up, laughed and shouted, 'Hey, Wally, I can see your ash-pan'. Well that did it! He turned and seized this young lad, laid him across his knee and whacked him hard – so hard indeed that the offender bellowed his eyes out in the hedge bottom for the next half hour. However the harm was done and the word soon went round all the farms and everyone was asking him 'Wally, seen any good ash-pans lately?' He stuck this teasing for several weeks but it got more than flesh and blood could stand and one morning he appeared with the seat of his trousers mended. He'd cobbled the tears together with string on one side and darning wool on the other cheek with stitches about an inch long – no longer could anyone claim to see his ash-pan.

7.

GRANDPARENTS, AND THE CIRCUS

I CAN JUST REMEMBER, before we had a car, our weekly trips on the old motor cycle and then one day I realised Mother thought she had moved up the social scale when Dad purchased his first motor car. This was a navy blue, bull-nosed Morris. We all gathered to look this over in speechless admiration. Even though it looked very much the worse for wear, chipped paintwork, bald tyres and other signs of age, it worked. We all piled into the vehicle in great excitement – Dad sitting by the mechanic so that he could see what wanted doing to make the thing move. He soon mastered the art and we graduated from the Home Field on to the road! Along we chugged in clouds of dust and steam until Dad held he was quite proficient in the art of driving. Then the mechanic showed Dad where to put in oil and water; explained the bat-

tery to him, retrieved his bike which had been strapped on the back, waved cheerio and left. Ten minutes later he dashed back, very sorry, but he'd forgotten to give Dad a lesson in reversing!

We had many happy times in that car – our fortnightly visits to our Grandparents when practically every trip was marked by a puncture. The canvas showed through all the tyres and we also frequently ran out of petrol as no-one could prevail upon Dad to buy more than one gallon of petrol at a time – he thought it was a waste of money if we didn't actually need it then. One never to be forgotten summer when harvest was over early Dad took his courage in both hands, bought more than one gallon of petrol, invested in four re-conditioned tyres and set off, complete with family, for a holiday in Suffolk, my mother's home.

We chugged along very carefully, and after one break for a picnic we arrived safely at my uncle's house. He worked on the railway and lived in a small cottage by the station. This we all thought was lovely, used to space and a large farm house as we were, it was like living in a doll's house, great fun. The grown-ups were probably not quite so enthusiastic!

About a quarter of a mile from Uncle's house was the river Stour – and as water was strange territory to us we explored this new dimension. We spent hours playing on the sands; scrambling over the wreck of a large coaster that had been driven ashore years before; eating shrimp paste sandwiches with so much sand in them that they gritted on the teeth. Sometimes we even persuaded the grown-ups to paddle with us and on one memorable day Uncle agreed to go bathing with us and to teach us to swim. I shall never forget the sight of him as he emerged from behind a sand-dune, complete with bathing costume that had arms and legs in it! We were all so rude, falling about with laughter that it's a wonder he came into the water with us.

One day we decided to venture further afield for a picnic in Constable country. My mother's family were all brought up at Flatford and East Bergholt. The food was packed and we all piled into the car. We explored the Mill and jumped off the bridge into the water below and thoroughly enjoyed ourselves playing in the water like puppies. Eventually we moved off and found a suitable field for a picnic, where we spread out the cloth, put the food down and settled to enjoy ourselves, eating, gossiping and generally relaxing. Our elders settled down for a quick snooze and we children were so replete with food that we were too lazy for any mischief. Suddenly the peace of the afternoon was shattered as Frank lept to his feet with a frantic yell. He'd chosen an ant-hill. He soon found it was an active ant-hill; he was covered with the insects practically to his waist – and rushing around and tearing off his trousers he screamed for help. Unfortunately he was running so fast no-one could catch up to help him. Eventually Mother quietened him and de-anted him and his trousers – poor lad he was in a mess, Ray and I felt quite sorry for him when we could stop laughing.

My Lincolnshire grandad was a most amiable character though I gather from family gossip he was a reformed rake! From the family legend we were told that his father was a cattle dealer. He married the daughter of a wealthy jeweller against her parents' wishes; this result-
ed in her being 'cast-out' by her father's family with a dowry of one hundred pounds – in the best Victorian tradition! The marriage, we are led to believe, was full of incident – the husband was finally killed in a drunken brawl. His wife had her baby early as a result of the shock and

died in childbirth or very soon after.

The baby, Jabez, my grandfather, was brought up by a woman in the village who was notorious for smoking a clay pipe and swearing like a man! However she must have had a heart because she kept his mother's £100 intact for the baby and when old enough encouraged him to work on a farm in a village near Lincoln before becoming proficient enough to rent a farm for himself.

When Grandfather was in his twenties he married a blacksmith's daughter. Now Jabez was like his father—he drank heavily. Grandmother Eliza stood this for some time but one day she confronted him when he returned home drunk from market. What she said or did history does not relate but from that day he never touched another drop of liquor. He brewed the ale for the men at harvest time but never even tasted it himself. Indeed his reformation was such that he took to religion—Methodism, of course. A few years later he became a lay preacher and walked miles every Sunday on the circuit to preach in the surrounding villages.

I remember him as a lovable old man – he sat in his Windsor

chair and smoked his pipe so energetically that his head was permanently enveloped in a cloud of smoke. He had a very ready sense of humour – he would sit in his chair – tears of laughter rolling down his face – his body shaking from head to feet, but not a sound came from him. All his grandchildren loved to watch this phenomenon. The last occasion on which I saw him was rather sad. He had gone to visit his elder daughter who was a houseproud tyrant. As it was snowing she made him sit in a chair with his feet in a wooden box so that her carpet should not be dirtied.

Our family visited Granny and Grandad every second Sunday. If the weather was bad Granny always sent Dad to pick up his father from whichever chapel he happened to be preaching in. Invariably Grandad refused the lift as he didn't trust these machines. He then silently walked home, Dad accompanying him in the car, driving along in first gear, side by side! In the Easter holidays I was sometimes left behind on one Sunday to be picked up by my parents when they next visited. As my favourite food at that time was 'Camp' coffee and bread and cheese I don't think I caused too much work.

Every night before we went to bed Grandad read a chapter of the Bible aloud to Granny – when I was there I was allowed, as a great privilege, to take over this task. I felt very proud and grown-up as it was truly the highlight of their day.

I slept in a beautiful, soft, voluminous feather bed that I usually sank in, almost out of sight. At bedtime Granny solemnly took the copper warming pan off the wall and put it on the fender in the hearth in front of the fire. It was then opened up to receive the glowing coals. Granny got the raker and pulled the fire apart until she found the right hot cinders – then she shovelled them out, put them in the warming pan and closed it. We would both go straight upstairs and I used to watch fascinated as she leisurely stroked the pan up and down beneath the sheets to warm the bed. She'd then flip the clothes back and tell me to hop in. As a great luxury I was allowed to say my prayers in bed.

Granny always dressed in black and wore what were called 'ward shoes', flat black strapped shoes worn I suppose by the

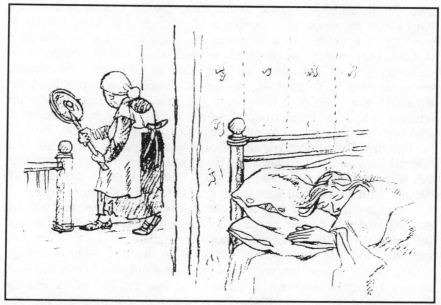

early nursing orders. On a Sunday in summer or at a family wedding she would occasionally wear a lavender-coloured dress, with a black shawl draped over her shoulders. To me, an uncritical audience, she had all the solid Victorian virtues and none of the vices. She really did love her neighbour as herself. One last note about Granny; she was the best pastry maker any of our family have ever come across – her puff pastry really did melt in one's mouth.

I remember my other grandad coming to see us only once – he preferred to stay at home and his family had to visit him. He was an East Anglian farmer who lived for his horses and his ploughing, winning many trophies – both county and national. He really was a relic of a by-gone age, distrusting anything new. He grew a long white beard and talked with a very thick accent, using words which sounded to us like 'nooit' 'tooit' and 'ferruk', i.e. night, tight and fork. We could scarcely understand him and I suppose it was the same in reverse. Surprisingly my mother had very little accent, probably because she'd worked as a lady's companion and had served in the Royal Flying Corps in the First World War, consequently moving and mixing with many people.

The one time Grandad came to stay with us we children walked very warily as he had a somewhat hasty temper and children should definitely be seen and not heard – he should know as he'd had eight! He was most suspicious of our food, he wouldn't eat anything that was not instantly recognisable for what it was, no made-up dishes for him. Mother, thinking to give him a treat and a change from the everlasting bacon, bought for the first time some breakfast cereal called Post Toasties! She offered him them; he looked at them most suspiciously and said 'Ah don' eat pigs' whittles woman!' She was quite deflated; we didn't mind though, we ate them and thought they were great.

About this time I moved from the school in the next village and attended a junior school in Sleaford. Dad had high hopes for me and decided I needed more competition. I think he saw me fulfilling the ambitions he'd had for himself – he'd always wanted to be a teacher, with history as his subject. He's the only person I know who'd read Gibbon's *Decline and Fall of the Roman Empire* and H. A. L. Fisher's *History of Europe* purely for pleasure— he was a voracious reader. Anyway I duly settled into my new school and made friends and thoroughly enjoyed the wider scope of subjects offered. My brother Ray gave me a lift in the morning on the crossbar of his bicycle and in the afternoon I walked home as the boys stayed late for football.

Now I suppose I had bragged about the farm and the animals and all the antics we got up to, for one day three of my friends decided to walk home with me and see for themselves if it was all true. Having settled this among ourselves with no thought for their non-appearance at home, and certainly no thought for worried parents, we set off. We employed my usual trick for covering the three and a half miles quickly; we walked from one telegraph pole to the next, then ran to the next, walked to the next and so on and were soon home. Mother was very surprised to see all the girls but assumed it was all done with approval so sent us into the yard while she prepared a bumper tea. We played with the cats and dogs, talked to the piglets and calves and finally walked down the fields to say 'hello' to Tommy. We returned and sat down to a lovely tea with all the family, when we were interrpted by Jim barking in the yard and the sound of irate voices and bicycles being propped against the barn wall. Three men then walked along the yard and grimly surveyed us through the open kitchen door; retribution had caught up with us! They were furious as they'd had to track down other friends, go to other houses to find out where their daughters had disappeared to. It took all Mother's charm and plenty of cups of tea and food, to placate them. We were all thoroughly scolded for our thoughtlessness and promised never to do it again unless our parents knew. We got together at school next day and really couldn't see what all the fuss was about; the days of being warned about getting into cars with strange men mercifully hadn't arrived.

Friends and relations often came to stay in the summer months, especially at harvest time. This was encouraged by my dad who considered it a form of cheap labour as all but the really elderly had a pitchfork put into their hands as soon as they appeared in the stackyard to have a look around. There were always loose-boxes which needed cleaning out; hen-huts to be mended, or Tommy to be taken to the blacksmith—if he felt like being taken! No one seemed to mind these jobs, indeed they appeared to like joining in and as they were well-fed they left us fitter, leaner and happier—a health farm with a difference. However, one of my mother's brothers and his family decided to brave the cold, searing Lincolnshire winds and come for a week at Christmas. We children were delighted at the thought of more kindred spirits at the festive season, visions of party games floated before us, as well as more nefarious pranks!

Mother put the turkey plucking and dressing forward by a couple of days, no doubt praying for the cold weather to continue to keep the birds fresh; the mincepies, cakes and other goodies were all prepared well in advance. That just left the bedrooms to be prepared. Now all our bedrooms, except that of the boys, had one thing in common – they had limestone floors, fairly common in farmhouses of that age. These made the rooms very cold in winter, especially as most of them just had the occasional hand-made rag-rug by the bedside. Of course, we were so used to these conditions that we didn't notice; we accepted the fact that the water in our wash-stands would be iced over in the mornings.

When Mother entered the big bedroom allotted to my aunt and uncle, even she decided it might seem a trifle spartan for their southern comfort. The windows were checked for broken glass but for once all the panes were intact. It was some months since we'd put a ball through any window except those of my bedroom. When that happened we just put a piece of cardboard in to keep the wind and rain out. As it was my bedroom that suffered most – and became progressively darker – it was considered my own fault and nothing was done until Dad had his annual 'window day'. Once a year he went round and put in fresh glass and putty where necessary – he always meant to paint these repairs but never did, so our house always had a slightly piebald appearance. But I digress! Mother washed and polished the room, fetched the best pieces of furniture from her own bedroom to improve it, but it still felt icily cold. After due consideration she decided that there was only one thing for it, she must put a fire in the grate! That was an almost unheard-of luxury– one had to be really ill to warrant heating a bedroom.

So, as soon as she'd finished all her polishing, she fetched paper, sticks, wood and coal, sank to her knees and laid the kindling. All went well for a few seconds then, as the flames really caught hold and smoke poured up the chimney, disaster struck: the smoke gushed greedily back into the room completely enveloping my mother. As a spectator, I thought this highly amusing; Mother, at this stage not unduly worried, thought it merely the gusting wind playing in the chimney and having a laugh at our expense, but no, it was more serious than that. Smoke continued to pour back. Mother could not understand it – the chimney did not need sweeping as she knew that room hadn't had a fire for twenty years to her knowledge. She tried vainly to put the fire out, but having once caught hold it was not letting go so easily. Finally, in exasperation, she threw up the sash window and with the aid of fire-tongs and shovel she threw the whole lot out of the window onto the front garden.

The room was by now a frightful mess. I was told to start

cleaning up while she fetched Dad in to sweep the chimney: the penny had finally dropped – 'the dratted jackdaws', they'd nested there, why they had to do that when there were plenty of good trees out, she didn't know. I'd swept and dusted again before Dad arrived, complete with brushes and rods, grumbling at having been fetched in from his work. But time was getting short; the relations were to be fetched from the station in about an hour's time, so – get on with it, please!

Dad knelt down and peered up the chimney: all was black, not a speck of daylight to be seen at the top of the straight stack. However, 'I'll soon settle this' said Dad, 'Ray, go out into the garden and tell me when the brush comes out'. Screwing the brush onto the first group of rods, Dad pushed the contraption upwards. I was shoo'ed to the window to relay Ray's signal but that was premature: Dad came to a full stop, not one inch further could he go. After much puffing and panting, he sat back on his heels and considered the situation. He opined that he'd get more purchase on the rods if he sat with his back to the firegrate and heaved the rods up over his shoulder. This he did, heaving and straining, becoming redder with the effort until finally something gave: there was a rumbling, rushing and

 scraping which seemed to go on for ever. Rivetted to the grate, I watched my dad look enquiringly upwards . . . what a mistake! Twigs, old bird's nest, bits of tin and glass, metal wire, cow dung, slivers of brick and mortar, bird's bones, the accumulated detritus of twenty years cascaded down the chimney and buried him.

Slowly the filth settled; the heap of rubbish stirred, and a black face peered out at us. The tension was broken by Ray, shouting with great excitement: 'The brush is out, the brush is out'! We smiled, we giggled, hysterical laughter took us all—we were helpless. Dad said not a word; he stood up very slowly, shook the worst off himself, glowered at each and every one of us and majestically stumped off downstairs. We dried our eyes, laughter subsided and we gazed around at the havoc. Once again the window was thrown up, the rubbish shovelled up and thrown into the garden, bedclothes changed, new counterpane laid neatly. For the third time the room was swept, cleaned, dusted; and re-polished. With a pause like a genuflection, my mother went once more on hands and knees and lit the fire. Soon a cheerful blaze made the room welcoming and gave an appearance of warmth.

Our relatives arrived five minutes after the room was finished. My aunt and uncle were loud in their appreciation of the kindness shown; they wouldn't have brought all those extra woollies and bedsocks if they had known. I must admit they did look a little sideways at our grubby appearance, and the traces of soot on Mother's face. Dad maintained a lofty silence and apparent detachment throughout supper.

As, apart from one or two toddlers, I was the only girl in the village, I relied on the boys for companionship. They were quite good about it and I was accepted into the village gang. As I was a faster runner and better at catching balls than most of them, I don't think I was too much of a drawback. However, accept me they did and I was allowed to take part in all the mischievous activities.

On many a summer evening we would all sit on the banks of the beck and gather ten pebbles each. We then had a competition, seeing who could score the most hits on the ceramic pots on the telegraph poles; if we shattered them we got two points. All this was strictly umpired and the winner was allowed to nominate the next game. No one was concerned about the ethics of this exercise, after all, we didn't have one telephone in the village so why should we bother. All went well until one day a postman, obviously lying in wait behind a hedge, jumped out at us. One of the boys in his anxiety to get away jumped off the side of the bridge over the beck and broke his leg. The village parents then united, at the instigation of the post office, and barred this amusement.

Of course in the winter, under cover of darkness, our ingenuity had free reign. One of the cottages was occupied by a family called Jackson and the man of the house was called 'The General'. This may have been a throwback from the American General Jackson, but I doubt whether anyone was well-enough read to think that up: it was probably that he just looked like one— over six feet tall, very upright with white hair and moustache. Be that as it may, we did seem to pick on his cottage for our bit of fun.

One Hallowe'en we decided to make turnip-head masks, so the whole gang went into my dad's crew yard and selected a good-sized turnip each. Then we all produced our knives and started to whittle away at the flesh on the inside; that done we cut out the eyes and grinning mouths. I was deputed to slip into the house to see if I could find the odd spare candle. I openly asked Mother for some and she quite unsuspectingly gave me one, no doubt thinking mask-making was a fairly harmless pastime. When I returned with the candle the boys had had a good idea – the two lads who lived next door to the Jacksons had noticed that a pair of The General's overalls were still out on the clothes line, no doubt because they were frozen solid. We crept stealthily and with great difficulty prised the overalls free. We put the end of a yard brush through the bottom of the mask, slipped the other end down the overalls, propped the whole thing against a gooseberry bush near the back door, lit the candle and retired quickly. My elder brother crept along the path, knocked loudly on the door and then shot off round the other side of the cottage. When Mrs Jackson opened the door and saw the leering figure wearing her husband's overalls her resulting hysterics were very satisfying.

High-flown with the success of this venture the next brilliant idea was to fill a long tin with cold water, balance this on the head of a brush which was then balanced upside down against the door. Again the boys knocked and ran. This time the General, probably to spare his wife, opened the door himself so that he received the benefit of all the water which cascaded over

him. He spent half the night roaming the lanes, with his stick, in pursuit of the taunting owl hoots. I think that all male parents received official complaints from the poor man – anyway both my brothers received a sound thrashing from Dad and we all had to stay in every night for a month. I didn't get beaten because Dad couldn't believe that I'd lend myself to anything like that. I know that Dad gave the Jacksons many a rabbit after that and the other children's dads sent vegetables and fruit.

During the long summer evenings we constructed a sledge on wheels from bits of old prams and attached some rope on the front to steer it. Then we took it in turns to sail down the hill and round the corner at the bottom. We got up a fair turn of speed and sometimes instead of negotiating the corner we went straight over the bank and finished up head first in the nettles. This was one of our more harmless pursuits, until the day we met a lorry coming round the corner and up the hill. That was the day we discovered the steering mechanism was not to be relied upon. The lorry driver, taking evasive action, left the road and ended up in the dyke on the other side of the road. I was quite shocked by his language, it enlarged my vocabulary considerably.

Living on a farm I was always aware of the mating and birth of animals, as I was of the death of animals. So when I heard the stallion was to pay us a visit I only gave the news passing interest. The afternoon arrived and I, with all the rest, gathered round to admire him. He was a splendid animal who certainly knew his own worth. Over a ton of gleaming chestnut bone and muscle. His mane and tail were braided with bright ribbons, his leathers and brasses were polished to perfection, even his hooves and shoes were burnished. As he walked along his well-brushed feathers floated in the air and every bell on his proudly-arched back tinkled with each step— a magnificent sight. In contrast his owner, Mr Chalmers, was quite tiny and seemed to hang on to the leading rein by kind permission of the horse, who every so often broke into a prance at the thought of his afternoon's work; he was certainly the dominant partner in that relationship.

My dad duly directed him to a corner of the Levels where 'Dinah' the Shire mare was awaiting his attentions. Suddenly Dad noticed me and told me to go into the house with Mother. Why was I being excluded when my brothers were allowed to remain? It wasn't fair, I thought to myself, why the mystery? I had only to look out of the kitchen window any day of the week to see the cockerels mating with hens, ducks being chased, shrilly quacking in protest, by amorous drakes. To say nothing of the pigs, sheep and, every now and then, the bulls and heifers in the home field – so why the banishment? I was puzzled.

Suddenly I thought I'd got the answer— there must be a different way of doing it. By now I was burning with curiosity so as soon as Mother left the kitchen on one of her numerous tasks I slipped out and went up the stairs, along the landing, up the next stairs into the attics. One of the windows directly over-looked the field of operations so I had a grandstand view of the proceedings. Just the same as usual. What was all the fuss about? Just then I heard mother's voice demanding to know my whereabouts so I slipped quickly down the stairs, missing the two that creaked, and ran across the landing into my bedroom. By the time Mother's enquiring head came round the door I was lying flat, face down on my bed, kicking my legs, head propped on hands, absolutely lost to the world in *Kidnapped*. At the time I had such a job to keep my look of innocent frustration in place – it required great concentration in view of the meaningful self-satisfied smirks I got from the boys.

One of the highlights of our year was the visit of the circus to Sleaford. The children at school talked of nothing else for weeks beforehand. It was inconceivable that there should be anyone who couldn't go. The boys and I started our campaign very early, as soon as the advance notices were posted. To start with we made comments to one another – to test the water, so to speak. It would be no good making a real effort if our parents decided it was a necessary evil they had to put up with anyway.

It wasn't. Dad said we hadn't any good money to throw away on circuses, if there was any money to spare he'd buy another calf to feed. We said we'd all get in for 1/6d and calves cost more than that. Battle was joined. We offered to shut the chickens up at night for a whole month without grumbling. We offered to cut, wash and bunch watercress from the beck and send it to the market. We offered to go to Sunday School every week and come back clean. We offered to wash the causey outside the back door every Saturday. Oh, how we offered. Eventually we wore them down and they agreed we could go. At least Mother and we three would go; Dad would take us on the motorbike and side-car which we had at that time, and then do a round of all the local agriculture machinery firms and price new canvasses for the binder. Harvest would soon be here and on inspection the old binder canvasses were so old and mended that there was nowhere to which the leather straps could be stitched.

The great day dawned and we set off in high fettle, chugging along on the old Norton, Ray riding pillion behind Father, Mother with me on her lap in the side-car and Frank crouched on the floor between her feet. Dad left us after agreeing to pick us up two hours later. We walked up to the field and joined the queue, waiting to pay. Frank wanted to make a deal with Mother – could he go round to the back of the tent and crawl in under the canvas – then he could spend his 2d on sweets. Mother firmly forbade this, I'm sure she couldn't face the indignity of being recognised as his mother when he was caught, as he surely would be, otherwise at least 50% of the other children present would have tried it.

We settled in our seats and it was pure bliss. The enormous elephants lumbered round – lifted up their feet, all trumpeted together, they stood up on their hind legs – then trunks holding tails they walked out. Two sad sea-lions balanced balls on their noses: elegant horses in fine trappings cantered round with buxom lasses in spangles standing on their backs; clowns fell over, lost their trousers, hit one another, fell into the audience and generally created mayhem. Finally, the moment we had all been waiting for – the trapezes were let down from the roof – the safety nets were put in position and the drums began to roll. Our eyes were lifted, our breath was held and we 'ooh'd and ahh'd' at each flight. It was pure magic.

When we arrived home the boys were very thoughtful and whispered together in corners – next day they disappeared for long stretches at a time. I eventually tracked them down in the large crew yard. As it was summer all the cattle were out in the fields so we had the place to ourselves. Half of the yard was covered by a high tin roof held in place by substantial beams. Brother Ray was crawling along one of these and tying on two lengths of wagon rope. These were then knotted round an old fork handle and – hey presto – there was our very own trapeze. We all tried it very gingerly at first but it seemed quite secure. Father came along and pulled and tugged and pronounced it to be quite safe so long as we didn't fall off sideways on to the stone water trough. We spent hours and hours on that contraption, getting more and more daring. We went so high we were in danger of hitting the roof – we all learned to hang upside down, with our ankles wrapped around the ropes, arms stretched wide, calling ourselves the Flying Angels.

Later on in the year when the cattle were brought in it became even more of a challenge. To start with, the straw underneath the trapeze was not so clean as it had been. Also the cows were overcome with curiosity at the sight of bodies flying through the air. We eventually had to make the rule that no-one used the equipment unless the other two were there to keep the cattle away in line at the side. They used to stand there, great big placid eyes looking in curiosity at us, their tails occasionally swishing in what we took to be applause. The sight of all the horns underneath was quite intimidating, one didn't want to come off and be speared by a Lincoln Red!

The next challenge was to see how high up we could be before we let go of the bar in order to land on our feet. We got so expert at this that Frank suggested one day that we should hold a cow in line with the bar but facing away from us and see if we

68.

could land astride the animal. After a bit of thought Ray took Frank on one side and they had a whispered conversation, then told me they couldn't do it as they might damage their anatomy. However Frank dared me to do it as I was built differently! One of the few dares I refused! How was I to be certain they'd have the cow in the right place at the right time?

Why we never killed or seriously injured ourselves I'll never know. Ironically the one real injury was caused when Frank was where he should be, doing the task he was asked to do. Dad had a small mill which was run by a petrol-driven engine joined to it by a belt. One day Dad asked Frank to put the last few buckets of corn through as we were short of milled barley for the chicken mash. A few minutes later we heard yells of agony – of course we all rushed to the barn and found Frank crying – blood everywhere! He had tried to flick the last few grains down the chute and had caught his little finger in the machinery – this had taken the end clean off.

Mother rushed into the house and brought out a clean towel to wrap round the hand – Dad put him on his cross-bar and cycled like mad to the doctor in the next village, two miles away. Ray and I were quite upset by this and wandered off together. I asked Ray if he thought it was bad and he said he thought it was as he could see the bone. We ghoulishly decided to look for the finger-end; we couldn't find it so decided one of the farm cats had got there first. An hour later Dad arrived home again with Frank who acted the wounded hero with great conviction; he was too ill (so he said) to undertake any of his usual tasks about house and yard. He demonstrated how his accident happened as often as we'd let him and we all had to count his stitches many times. His finger finally healed in such a shape that it became quite useful in opening locks.

On market days, tea was always an enjoyable affair. If we'd had a good day and the rabbits had made a penny or two more each, or the blackberries had fetched a good price, then we would have a treat! Sometimes it was a few shop-bought currant buns to toast at the kitchen range, or, if it had been a truly good day, we had the ultimate feast—a pork pie! How we loved them, fresh from the butchers. We never knew until the food was actually brought to the table what Monday tea would consist of. Of course, we pestered Mum and asked what was for tea. Why we bothered I don't know for we always got the same reply, 'Bread and pullet'. That was her stock answer to any query about food: where the phrase came from I never discovered – from her own childhood memory I suppose.

After lashings of bread and butter; pork pie (if we were lucky) and cake – which was not appreciated as it was home-made – we would then sit round the kitchen table, push aside plates and cups and saucers, and swap the day's experiences. This was my Dad and Mum's one great contact with the outside world. Mother would gossip about the other wives she'd met; what they were wearing, what was on the stalls in the market, who was buying what and for how much, and who'd got what the matter with them. Any little tit-bits would be mulled over and the last little bit of interest extracted.

'Well, Father, who've you seen today?' Then Dad would go through his cattle market experiences, moment by moment. No scandal here of course, all solemn, serious farming business; men had no time for lighter, social chat. The fact that he always knew which farmer had been relegated to the 'gander-pen' was quite incidental. It was years before I realised the meaning of this expression.

8.

THE DEPRESSION YEARS

L IFE WAS NOT ALWAYS A GREAT SOURCE OF FUN and enjoyment. I remember one very sad time when everything seemed to be depressing and dull. During the Thirties life was, in farming as in many other occupations, very very hard.

I do not, of course, remember the General Strike, as I was only a few months old. As our farm had neither gas nor electricity, no water laid on, and a cess-pit did the duty of sewage pipes, I suppose it would pass by almost unnoticed. Certainly the lack of postal service was no hardship, that merely meant that the bills could not be delivered! I'm sure my parents would have realised that it was taking place but its impact would have been minimal.

Not so the Depression: that was years of hardship and deprivation that slowly ground down the people of the industrial North and the Midlands. It ate into their minds and souls, destroying hope, sapping initiative, starving minds as well as bodies. It destroyed whole communities and scattered families, creating wounds and scars from which many did not recover. I do remember a feeling of near-despair in our own home, when money was virtually non-existent. Farm produce prices tumbled but it was always supposed that everything would improve next year. No one in my family foresaw the depth of the Depression nor the length of time it would last. I'm sure even my father would have voted differently if he had realised all the implications. We were lucky in a way I suppose in that we children were very young and made no very great demands on our parents. I know they worked practically every hour that God gave in order to survive the Depression. It seemed that every day we heard of neighbouring farmers going bankrupt and selling up, their implements very nearly given away as everyone else was in the same boat, with not a halfpenny to spare.

We lived on wild rabbits; as Dad couldn't spare any money

for cartridges we ferretted them or set snares. Much as we liked roast rabbit it grew very monotonous, month in and month out, only relieved by fat bacon for breakfast. These two with home-made bread, milk, cheese and apples, and blackberries formed our diet, probably very healthy but we did long for a bit of beef sometimes. When we had baker's bread it was a real treat. I well remember the day my dad came into the kitchen to ask for the egg money to pay Owd Sam; Mother handed him her purse without a word and he carefully emptied it out on the kitchen table and counted out 32s.6d. This he collected up and went into the yard to give it to Sam. When he had gone Mother picked up her purse and held it upside down and one halfpenny dropped out. She said, with tears rolling down her cheeks, 'That's all the money we've got in the world, I don't know where any more will come from.'

We did survive, selling everything we could lay our hands on; hazelnuts from the hedges, blackberries and watercress from the beck. We got up early to gather mushrooms for the stalls— anything we could think of. One farmer we knew well in the next village hanged himself in his own barn.

The wages of farm labourers went down from 38/6 per week to only 27/6 per week. Hundreds walked from farm to farm, village to village looking for non-existent work— what a reward for fighting for your country! My dad was very soft-hearted and when these gaunt figures appeared in the stackyard and always asked the same question, 'Any work for me, maister? Gie us a job!', he would dearly have liked to have given every one a job. Goodness knows, his own work-load was horrendous but he had no money with which to pay them. His reply was always the same, 'Sorry, not at the moment, sorry. Go to the kitchen door and see if the missus has got a cup of tea on the go'. Of course, she usually had.

We always had the tramps or 'shag-ans' as we called them calling at meal times. There we were, sitting round the kitchen table with the door always propped open when Jim, lying across the doorway, would begin to growl. Everyone would stop eating and watch the kitchen window: eventually a shadow would go by and then materialise near the doorway too afraid of the growling dog to come near enough to knock. Then came the dreaded question and the equally dreaded answer. The shag-ans always carried a tin can for tea, so while my mum filled up their billy-cans ladling in the sugar without question, my Dad would silently cut two thick slices of home-made bread, a thick slice of fat bacon which he slapped between the slices and then silently handed it to the man when he got his billy-can back. There would be a muttered, 'God bless you, maister', and off they'd trudge to the next farm.

If it was near night, the tramping men would ask if they could sleep in the barn. Permission was always given with the added rider: 'No smoking in there, mind!' After a time the condition was dropped; who had fags anyway? By the time you were around the next morning, there would be a round indentation in the hay or straw but the travelling man would be gone— hoping to be the first to ask at the next farm. Of course, if they could find the odd egg, a few apples or turnips to take with them for their next meal, shoulders were just shrugged but the food was never grudged.

Sometimes my mother would try to talk to them and find out where they'd come from, but the utter hopelessness of their replies, particularly when talking of wives and families, was sadness personified. A few said their families had gone to their parents or other members of the family who had work, but they had been away so long they really didn't know what had happened to them. There were no government aid schemes or soup kitchens in the villages but we all looked after our own without question, even if a spot of poaching or thieving was necessary to do it. We knew our absentee landlords were not going hungry. Sometimes we did have casual work to offer in potato harvest or beet time, and then things cheered up. The casuals were able to go home with a little money for their families.

New clothes were out of the question, one just patched up what one had and hoped the children didn't grow too much. I well remember my second brother's fury because he always had to have my elder brother's hand-me-downs. Why couldn't he have something of his own? It didn't seem to penetrate that I wore the trousers out round the farm – at third hand! However, Frank had his laugh over Ray when things got so bad for school clothes that Mother decided to make a coat and trousers for Ray out of the best bits of Dad's old jackets. The trousers weren't too bad; a bit cobbled up around the seat but at least wearable. The jacket, however, was a disaster! The pattern in the material went one way on one sleeve and the opposite on the other: the lapels were abandoned altogether. The result was dreadful to behold and Ray flatly refused even to try it on. When Mother said it would have to do for school, he yelled, he pleaded, he sulked and generally created mayhem. Eventually my dad intervened and said he'd have to make do with just his pullover and macintosh. A good thing too, as I'm sure the hated garment would never have got beyond the stackyard! It finished life, incidentally, as a very dull part of a kitchen snip-rug.

Keeping our feet dry was another difficulty. In the summer we just put layers of paper inside our shoes over the holes and hoped it didn't rain. We found the tough, blue sugar bags best for this; sometimes they would last for two, even three days, before the paper needed renewing – especially if we'd managed to cadge a lift to school on a cross-bar or with Tommy in the milk-float. Winter brought more serious problems. Dad went to a sale and bought, for sixpence, an old cobbler's last; two sizes, one for grown-up, one for children's shoes. Thus set up he unearthed every old boot, every out-grown shoe and used these to cut out patches for our present footwear. I must admit he was quite handy at this and we usually had well-patched shoes though he was better with heels than soles which sometimes seemed rather knobbly on the inside. When Mother had blackened the boots and shoes they usually looked quite presentable.

We were very lucky I suppose in that we were never actually physically hungry. Hungry for a change of diet; for a few hours' rest from the eternal yard work; for relief from worry about where next quarter's rent money was coming from, but not hungry for food. A thirty stone fat pig takes a lot of eating: they produced only very fat bacon – about two inches of fat to a mere half inch, pink strip of meat. Still, it always went down with the help of boiled beetroot or pickled cabbage. Everything that could be picked and sold was picked and sold. My brothers and I spent one entire weekend picking, washing and bunching a particularly luxuriant crop of watercress that grew in our beck. It finally went to market with the eggs and butter, stacked in an old zinc bath and it fetched the princely sum of sixpence. We were disgusted!

On other occasions we picked blackberries by the can full and mushrooms by the basketful. If these matured other than on market days we used them for ourselves. One year there were mushrooms everywhere – so of course we ate them on every possible occasion. Now my Dad like his stewed in milk, then added flour which made a sauce. This I loathed: I cannot eat mushrooms to this day– to me they taste of earth and poverty. The boys and I grew adept at snaring rabbits– snaring was cheaper than shooting. The rabbits were then strung together in pairs for market. Mother always went along to the auction to see if the price was up a little on the previous week.

As the rent days came round, my dad became tense, sitting at the kitchen table with his two spikes for bills. He'd add them up again and again to make sure the figures were right. Usually there was a sigh of resignation and we'd know that he would have to sell a beast or two to augment the milk money to make the sum required. It was a happy day if we could manage without selling any stock. Such was the Depression.

9.

MY DAD DID NOT UNDERSTAND WOMEN

MY DAD DID NOT UNDERSTAND WOMEN. The workings of my mum's mind were a complete mystery to him. One could never accuse him of not trying but he seemed to have a genius for putting his foot in it and saying the wrong thing.

Take gardening for example. We had a large kitchen garden in which were grown potatoes, red beet, beans, peas, and carrots, and the general idea was that the men on the farm would do the heavy digging and weeding and Mother would plant the seeds and generally keep it tidy; Dad to help when needed. The understood thing was that the heavy digging was done on a wet day when the men couldn't do much on the farm or fill in the odd half hour before going home. This, of course, never seemed to happen and in desperation Mother would eventually take a spade and, every spare moment, she'd try and clean and dig a bit more.

Now my mum always suffered from a bad back to a greater or lesser degree and no doubt the digging aggravated it, so that one afternoon when she heard Dad and the two men laughing and talking before they went home, she really saw red and told him a few home truths about not doing his fair share. He was most apologetic and told her to leave the digging, he'd see it got done. Needless to say a week went by without another sod being turned. Again there were recriminations when Mother had to put in more spade work. This time Dad saw that she was really fed-up and had an aching back so at the week-end he had a token dig to keep the peace.

It so happened that it was Mother's birthday a day or two later and after breakfast Dad disappeared into Sleaford. He came in at dinner time holding a long, narrow parcel and looking very pleased with himself. 'You thought I'd forgotten your birthday, but I haven't. Here you are love, and many happy returns.' Mother looked surprised and very pleased and with

anticipation tore the wrapping from her birthday present. It was a new garden fork! I thought she would explode; even more so when he explained it was a lightweight version suitable for a lady's use and he thought it would make her digging easier. He couldn't see why she wasn't delighted with it.

Upon another occasion the following year they were invited to the wedding of a close friend. They accepted the invitation; Dad with resignation and Mother with pleasurable anticipation. Of course the question of what to wear soon arose—in Mother's mind anyway. Dad knew he'd got one suit and that, in his mind, was that. Mother gave her problem long and thoughtful consideration and decided that though she couldn't afford a new one, she would refurbish her best dress as well as she could. She decided to crochet a new collar and, as she was an expert at this art, she turned out a most beautiful creation with tiny butterflies clinging all the way round the edge. When this was put on to the dress it looked absolutely lovely.

So far so good, she decided she must have some new shoes. this was not surprising as every Sunday evening she had to scrub up her working shoes, leave them to dry overnight and then polish them up on Monday morning, ready to wear to market in Sleaford. She got out her carefully hoarded egg-money and decided she could buy the shoes and even a new hat. She had been saving up to buy another calf to feed but that would have to wait a little longer. Dad looked at her old patched shoes and agreed she really did need a new pair but why a hat, she already had one! Mother explained, very patiently, that her existing hat was navy blue and it went with her navy blue shopping coat and no, she couldn't possibly wear it with a brown and cream dress. Dad couldn't really see why not but decided to hold his peace.

Off to Sleaford she went and duly found herself a nice pair of shoes, just the right colour and of a sensible design that could eventually be demoted into working shoes. Following this purchase she found the best draper's shop in town, entered it and demanded to see their hats, something to match the brown shoes. She tried on the usual sort, sensible, no nonsense ones with brims and a ribbon or small feather to liven it up— all very disappointing. Half an hour later the assistant in desperation offered to show this recalcitrant customer the very latest designs that had, that week, just reached the shop. They were: 'Toques Madam, just like Queen Mary wears.' To the uninitiated toques were circular in shape and swathed in silk or tulle and very nonsensical and feminine. She produced one in cream and brown which Mother fell in love with. It certainly wasn't a marketing hat, a shopping hat or even an every Sunday hat, but it was the answer to every feminine urge she possessed at the moment! She recounted the egg money, consigned all her scruples to the Devil, took a deep breath, hoped there'd be other weddings, and bought it.

When we were all sitting round the tea-table that evening she casually announced she'd bought her hat and shoes and would

78.

anyone be interested in seeing them. Dad by now having his lines right said he would, in fact that's what he'd been waiting for. Mother retired upstairs and presently returned in refurbished dress and shoes. She was told she looked very sweet but where was the hat? With a determined expression on her face she once more retired to put on the hat, at the correct angle of course! She re-entered the kitchen and stood there with a defiant expression on her face. Dad took one unbelieving look, his eyes stood out like chapel hat-pegs, his mouth dropped open. We all watched with bated breath. 'Well', demanded Mother, 'what do you think?' Dad then uttered the immortal words, 'Eh, wuman, ye look a fairish heap in that.' We watched fascinated. Would she hit him, would she strangle him? No, she took the only course open to a woman, she burst into tears! Oh my poor father, how he did suffer! The only food and drink he obtained at the tea table was by courtesy of his offspring, for although Mother was assiduous in her attentions to us, nothing found its way up to his end of the table—and the frosty silence could be heard.

Two or three days later in a spirit of bravado Mother took herself off to the hairdresser and had her long hair (usually worn in a bun) cut and styled. She discovered to her amazement that her hair, relieved of its weight and with a bit of help from the hairdresser, waved and curled naturally – she became a curly dark blonde overnight – the toque did look good. Looking at photographs of the wedding in later years Mother really stole the show, she looked incredibly elegant. I do hope Dad appreciated this when he looked at her and didn't, in his mind's eye, bemoan the loss of that calf which never did scamper round the Home Field!

We all loved Jim, our collie; he was friend and playmate as well as a working dog. Inevitably of course, he grew old and grey about the muzzle. We began to realise his sight was failing and his hearing not so good. This was brought home to Dad one day when Jim, startled by the unheard approach of the postman, bit the inoffensive man. This was unheard of and the postman was understandably annoyed. A week later Ray was in the act of stepping over him and he was bitten also. It could no longer be ignored and one morning early my dad, very sorrowfully, removed him. None of us asked any questions but quite a gap was left in our lives.

We didn't replace him immediately as the wound was still too raw, but eventually Dad came in one day with a most beautiful Alsatian on a piece of rope. He was called Boxer and we quickly took him to our hearts, he had such a lovely nature. He was about a year old, only partially trained but a neighbouring farmer who had three or four dogs, on hearing of Jim's death, gave him to us. We were delighted with him; Dad had visions of completing his training, we had visions of a large friend and playmate.

One morning a very puzzled Mother came into the kitchen, she'd found egg shells on the lawn. Were the hens pecking their own eggs? A little covert observation revealed the dreadful truth to her, Boxer was stalking the hens and when they'd left their nests he went and helped himself to the eggs, carefully breaking the shells with his teeth then sucking up the contents. When Dad heard of the crime he was very cross with the dog and vowed to teach him a lesson, so he took him outside on to the grass, broke an egg in front of him, rubbed his nose in the resultant mess, then proceeded to belt the living daylights out of him. Boxer yelped and squirmed in distress but Dad really meant to teach him a lesson; eggs were too valuable a part of the family budget to be squandered in this way. Hopefully that would be that, but of course it wasn't. Although truly chastened, two days later he was discovered at his old tricks again – and again he was punished. Indeed by this time he was in such fear of Dad that as soon as he was in sight the dog retreated behind Mother for protection and if Dad glared at him he put his head down and whimpered in distress – indeed if no one else was about he would take refuge behind me – which was quite ridiculous as the dog was bigger than I was.

The third time he was seen to suck the eggs Mother decided to take a hand, a woman's more subtle approach was needed. She carefully opened a couple of eggs (cracked ones of course), mixed up a cupful of stiff mustard, filled the eggs, wiped them carefully and with three normal eggs put them back into the favoured nest. We sat back to await results. Next day, as no yelps of distress had been heard we went out to inspect the doctored eggs. These were found intact but the three good eggs were lying in the grass some distance away, merely empty shells. After a family conference it was decided, regretfully, that Boxer wasn't likely to be broken of this habit so he would have to be returned to our farmer friend. We were all very sorry about this as he was a lovely, lovable dog with this one fault in his make-up.

So, the next day Dad set off on his bike with the dog, firmly tied to a piece of rope, trotting along beside him. When he got to the farmyard Mr Foster smiled a little ruefully and said: 'Been up to his old tricks again has he, I'd hoped he'd give it up in a new home.' Dad was a bit cross and said he should have been warned, but Mr Foster had wanted him to have a fresh start. He explained to Dad that when Boxer was a young puppy he was a bit of a reckling so his wife had mixed raw egg in milk with a dash of brandy to give him a chance of survival. He'd thrived on this and developed a taste for it, too! Such a shame that kindness had had such results. We never heard what happened to him, but we knew he'd never survive long on a farm where there were chickens; it wasn't as great a crime as worrying sheep but getting on that way.

My dad was a Chapel-goer and my mum was Church of England but both attended with the other when in the mood. We children walked two miles to the next village, Ewerby, every Sunday morning, to attend Chapel Sunday School. I quite enjoyed this because I liked reading aloud and listening to the stories Mr Booth told us. Every summer we had an outing which consisted of dressing up a borrowed farm waggon with garlands of flowers and corn, putting in sheaves of corn for seats, donning our best clothes and Sunday faces, putting the horses in the shafts and setting forth. We had been practising our harvest hymns for many weeks as well as our recitations, and as we went round the nearby villages we'd stop and sing and recite at all the main points while the charity collectors would go round with tins. We loved this day and the sun always shone. I remember one day an old man came out of his house where he said his wife lay dying; he asked us to sing her favourite hymn. This we did and the superintendent said a few prayers. I hoped she could still hear us. I can still see that house, with the straw spread over the road to deaden the noise of the cartwheels. This seemed to be a common practice in our neighbourhood when someone was dying.

When we returned to the chapel about four hours later some of the mothers who lived nearby had covered the trestle tables at the back of the chapel, put out plates, cups and saucers and large plates of salmon sandwiches, jelly, bread and butter, and seed-cake on the tables, together with jugs of lemonade. I always tried to trade my seed-cake for an extra salmon sandwich as I didn't like the cake. As I had great difficulty doing this I suppose others felt the same.

Of course we didn't always arrive at Sunday School; sometimes other, more interesting things got in the way. We'd collect Beech nuts from the wayside trees and one warm Sunday morning Ray discovered a grass snake in the process of shedding its skin – this we had to watch in silent excitement and then, of course, it was too late to get there in time, so we played instead. We never got the prize for Best Attendance!

My Dad was a bit of a trial in church. It was quite remarkable but when we all went to chapel, he listened to the preacher and joined in the service. When we went to the village church he went to sleep. We always sat fairly near the back of the church, level with the organ so we certainly had plenty of noise but sure enough, without fail, once we settled back to listen to the vicar's sermon Dad began to nod. Mother would sit by his side, her back ram-rod straight and a determined, no-nonsense look on her face ready to deal with him if he dared to drop off again. He invariably did, starting with deep, regular breathing, then heavier still and suddenly the snores were there, reverberating gently round the back of the church. If Mother caught him before he got to the snoring stage a smart kick on the ankles was usually sufficient to bring him back, silently, to a sense of his surroundings – there was the odd occasion though when Mother got interested in the sermon and her watch over him wasn't sufficiently vigilant. He got away, his snores gathering momentum until he would choke himself awake and then he would invariably say: 'Eh, wots that, wot d'ye say?' in a loud voice. His resultant embarrassment was equalled only by Mum's, to the amusement of the rest of the congregation.

I remember another time in church when my dad caused my mother to vow she'd never go to church with him again. This was on the occasion of the marriage of a cousin some miles away in late September after the harvest was over. No farmers ever had time to marry during harvest time! As luck would have it major repairs were being undertaken in the church and there was a lot of scaffolding around. The good ladies who had decorated the church for the harvest festival the following day had shown initiative in using the scaffolding and had really made the place very beautiful, with corn, fruit, candles, and flowers in great profusion. We, dutifully clad in our Sunday best arrived in good time, sat down and surveyed the assembled throng, nodding and smiling at other friends and relations.

The bride duly arrived looking very happy and elegant and the service began. All went well and the ceremony was nearly over, the bride and groom were at the altar, listening to a homily on true love from the vicar. I was conscious of a slight stiffening of my mum's figure by my side – I looked along the pew and saw that my dad had helped himself to a handful of corn from the sheaf of wheat which adorned the end of the pew in front of him. He sniffed it, rubbed it between his hands to separate the chaff from the corn, blew the chaff away, sniffed the corn again and chewed it, giving it in fact, the full works. The chaff which he'd blown away with such indifference had settled coyly in the wide brim of the hat made of red straw, of the lady in front.

He then decided that the wheat in the sheaf behind him was of a different breed so needed to be assessed – more chaff in the red straw in front of him. By this time all eyes were upon him and one or two people were nudging one another and pointing at him – while he was quite unconscious of the interest he was arousing. Then he decided he'd better assess the merits of the corn on the scaffolding above his head – so he reached up, grabbed a handful and settled back in his seat again – Mother was, by this time, breathing fire and told him in no uncertain terms to 'have done'. He gave her an enquiring look as if to ask what all the fuss was about, then he proceeded to rub, sniff and chew this handful to see if it rated any higher than the previous two. By this time the red hat in front was really festooned with chaff in the flowers as well as the straw – mother got hold of his nearest hand and held it in hers firmly – one of his pals across the aisle leaned over and said in a penetrating whisper 'Got a good sample yet, Frank?' Dad looked up and suddenly became aware that he was the centre of interest and not the bride and groom. He went red with embarrassment, and subsided in his seat, not raising his eyes again until the happy couple passed by, never knowing they had been upstaged. When asked later by a farmer friend how the wheat rated in quality he said quite simply that it was not as good as his!

One day my dad had a letter from his bank manager asking him to call at the bank next time he was in town. This letter cast a gloom over everyone; was the overdraft higher than we'd supposed? Were they going to call in the bad debts? Dad hastily opened his drawer and got out all the bills, paid and unpaid, checked everything in the spike he kept on the kitchen dresser; nothing too outrageous came to light, what was the panic about? If the worst came to the worst, it was decided we could sell about three calves to offset whatever was causing the trouble, but that would be a pity as they weren't really ready for the market yet.

Anyway market-day came, Dad, done up in breeches and well-blacked leggings, set off and we settled down to wait as best we could. It was such a relief to see him come in with a wide smile on his face and to be told that unheard of thing, the Bank Manager was asking a favour of him. Apparently the manager's son, Roger, was away at school and needed a job of sorts to keep him occupied during the summer holidays. It wouldn't be necessary to pay him, (which was just as well), but he had no friends in the district as they'd only recently moved into our area and knowing Dad had two sons of around the same age, ie fourteen and fifteen, thought we'd be a good place for him to spend the holidays. It had been agreed that he should bike in every day, bringing his own food with him and work with us until tea-time. My dad felt quite smug about the fact he could do the powers that be a favour and no doubt reflected that it might give him a bit of leverage should that be necessary, in the future.

Roger duly arrived at the end of July. He was a big, strong, good-looking lad, with a well-modulated voice and no accent. Would we all get on well together? This seemed unlikely as to us he was 'posh' and anyone described as such we would inevitably view with some suspicion – but at the end of the first day he was declared to be a 'good-un', probably because he and Frank had a set-to over who was to drive the wagon home at night – Roger won. He seemed really to enjoy our kind of life, he entered into all the fun, abandoned bringing his own sandwiches and ate with us as he preferred Mother's cooking – this of course endeared him to her!

It soon emerged that it was a good thing we didn't have to pay him, however. Roger was, to quote my Dad: 'Uneppen wi' two left legs'. He was so clumsy that he was sometimes a danger to himself and, if he'd got a pitchfork in his hand, to everyone else as well. He was such a good-natured lad and he tried so very hard, but had really no aptitude whatsoever for harvest work. We soon accepted him as if he'd been one of the family for years, we teased him unmercifully of course, which he accepted with a good-natured smile. We soon learned not to enter into any verbal exchanges as he always won hands down – in fact he was a bright lad academically speaking.

Dad wouldn't trust him on the wagons, loading the sheaves of corn, as we knew that as soon as the horses moved forward anything above the sides of the wagons would immediately fall off – this sort of work was an art anyway – Dad did like the loads to be shipped up, that is the sheaves had to be arranged so that the load looked like the upturned keel of a boat. If this was well done the corn stayed in place without benefit of roping. So Roger, unable to do the more interesting jobs was given the job of 'picking', that is spearing the corn sheaves on the ground with his pitchfork and throwing them up to the 'loadener' so that he could put them in the correct place on the wagon. As he was so 'uneppen' Dad thought he'd better have him with his wagon – so Roger, with great enthusiasm, flung the corn up to him with great gusto, no time or rhythm about it whatsoever – sometimes he sent up two at a time, some would go right over and land on

the ground that had been cleared; others would land at the wrong end of the wagon and on several occasions he caught Dad on the back and indeed on one occasion he knocked him right off the load much to everyone's amusement. Dad was not happy!

When we got the corn into the yard and started to 'team' the loads to the people doing the stacking Dad decided that Roger would be best employed standing on the load throwing the corn down to the people building the stacks. That was an easy job, he couldn't possibly hurt himself or anyone else doing that. For some unknown reason Roger didn't realise that he was making life very difficult for himself if he stood on the actual corn he was trying to move! We couldn't believe it, there he was, legs firmly astride on the corn, tugging away like mad with his pitchfork at the sheaf between his feet, going red in the face from exertion. We fell about laughing, too breathless to explain to him why his efforts weren't paying off. Poor Roger, as I said, he'd no aptitude for the practical aspects of life.

We did love his company, his wit, his friendliness and thought we'd made a friend for life. Indeed he returned the following Christmas to see us and joined in the following harvest as well. To our eternal regret he was killed in the War on convoy duty in the Atlantic. What a waste of a super person!

To return to my dad and his problems. Following months of intermittent toothache he went – in sheer desperation – to the dentist. Regardless of what the poor man said my dad had decided to have every tooth out in one fell swoop, have a set of dentures made, and that would be that for evermore. This, against all advice, he proceeded to have done. What he hadn't reckoned with was that, whatever the dentist did, he could not make a set that was a good fit. Dad's new teeth had a life of their own! If they decided to be comfortable for a meal, then they would: if they didn't feel like it, they would almost drop out of their own accord.

As time went on, it was noticed that Dad was giving up the Battle of the Teeth. They were winning. Mother nagged and cajoled but Dad was wearing them less and less. Eventually only church and market days were teeth days, and then only if he'd had a square meal before he went – he couldn't face the challenge of eating in public. Who knew what the teeth would decide to do? Even on market days as often as not they would come home in Dad's pocket, wrapped in a clean handkerchief.

My mother had the bright idea of Dad wearing the o f f e n d i n g furniture at night when in bed, that way his mouth would get used to t h e m   w i t h o u t k n o w i n g

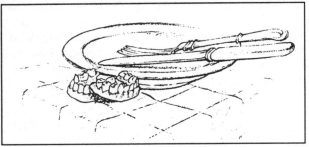

anything about it. After much badgering, Dad consented if only to keep his wife quiet. When he awoke next morning, he was without his teeth. Pandemonium reigned: not at the loss of the teeth but at the thought of where they might be. Dad was convinced he had swallowed them, and as they could not be found we all began to wonder if there might not be something in the idea.

Of course his caring family, instead of extending heartfelt sympathy and concern over his predicament, wondered aloud as to how far the teeth had penetrated. Would he require a doctor or a vet? We looked everywhere; we stripped the bed, we crawled under the bed, looked in all articles of bedroom equipment – to no avail. No pocket was unchecked; things were looked at, shaken and examined again – still no sign of the missing mandibles. Things began to look serious – had he really swallowed them? By now, my dad was beginning to look rather green with fright; so much so that Mother decided to make up the bed again – he looked as if he might need it. We shook, smoothed and folded in sheets and blankets. As Mother picked up the bolster for the umpteenth time the missing teeth shot out. Dad has obviously taken them out in his sleep and hidden them as far as he could reach in the bolster. Poor old Dad! He endured the ensuing teasing very well so relieved was he that he hadn't actually swallowed them.

The teeth came out again for church and Christmas and

then had a long rest. By now my dad's gums had hardened to such an extent that he didn't need teeth any more. However, they did have one more outing before being consigned to eternal rest. This was the occasion of my grandad's funeral.

My Dad's father died at the ripe age of 84: we'd loved him and expected to miss him. On the morning of the funeral, Dad was all ready to go, complete with teeth, when Jim growled and barked to warn us of strangers approaching. Dad went to investigate; had a quick word with the visitor, returned, paid the necessary call, and off we went. Five miles short of our destination, the dreadful truth was revealed in a solitary smile. From force of habit, Dad had removed his teeth for ease of conversation with a visitor and left them on the ledge by the kitchen sink. The ensuing row from the front of the car had to be heard to be believed! My mother opined that going to your own father's funeral minus teeth was showing a complete lack of respect: she would not be party to such behaviour . . . she would not attend a funeral with a man without teeth . . . what would folk think? Finally, in dire silence, the car was turned round and we chugged home to retrieve the dentures. Jim was the only one to show joy at our return, total bafflement at Dad's quick dash into the house, and he howled mournfully at our equally quick departure. We arrived in frosty silence, in time to join in the final hymn. When asked why we were late, my mother quickly responded that the journey had taken longer than she had bargained for, and my Dad snorted showing a double row of gleaming teeth. Grandad, who'd never been to a dentist in his long life, would have appreciated his son's dilemma!

Christmas was a time of mixed blessings. One of my mum's money spinners of the year was raising turkeys and dressing them ready for Christmas. She bought the turkeys from the hatchery as day-old chicks and cosseted them from the moment they arrived, about one hundred of them. She watched over them assiduously, and if one looked a little below par or, to quote her, a bit dicky, home remedies were soon applied. When they were babies Mother would hard boil eggs, all the cracked ones of course, allow them to cool and chop them up very finely to which she would add very finely chopped dandelion leaves – they used to thrive on this diet funnily enough. One of the remedies for off-colour young turkeys was to make them swallow a peppercorn – goodness knows what it did to their insides – frightened them into better health probably.

When they were old enough they would be moved to huts in the Home Field so that they had plenty of room. It was one of the prescribed jobs of us children to fasten the doors and hatches at night. We never skimped this job as rats were a menace and one had to be careful. I well remember one dreadful year in early December when the turkeys were plump and about ready for market; all the orders for Christmas had been taken and every one was booked. We'd had a good year and Mother had lost only about ten in infancy – so we'd ninety ready for selling – that money would buy spring pullets and also keep us in food for quite a long time.

Mother went to feed the turkeys in the morning and came back into the kitchen looking like death! Foxes had managed to get into the pens during the night and into the hut by an unnoticed hole in the rotten wood in the corner and driven the turkeys out and had killed over seventy of them. They hadn't killed them for food – only a few were mauled about – the rest had been killed just for sport. My dad hadn't really liked the Hunt coming on to his land previously, but after that they were welcome and if he heard a fox barking during the night he would get up and go after it with his gun. So much for the poor maligned fox.

In a normal year the turkeys were prepared for the customers during the week previous to Christmas. Dad and the men slaughtered the birds, and then everyone in the family donned their oldest clothes and we all repaired to an empty loose-box and began to pluck, frantically, far into the night by the light of paraffin lanterns. It was cold, miserable and itchy work as all the birds had fleas (their sort) on them. They certainly didn't live long on humans but were a nuisance while they lasted. As soon as about twenty birds had been plucked, and this had to be done very carefully so that the skin was not torn, Mother and I (when I was old enough) would repair to the kitchen and dress the birds, i.e. take out the innards, clean the giblets and truss the birds. A horrible job! After three days of this Dad and the boys would deliver them and collect the money. How we felt like eating our Christmas dinner I don't know, except that we had ducks.

Dad would cut a Christmas tree out from one of the plantations on the farm and we'd decorate it on Christmas Eve and put it in a place of honour in The Room. We didn't use The Room very often, only on high days, holidays and when we had visitors to stay. But at Christmas we went to town on it, we decorated it with paper streamers and great bunches of holly and mistletoe and we hung the cards everywhere, so that with a blazing log fire and candlelight it looked truly seasonal and lovely. The kitchen had to make do with Chinese lanterns made of paper with candles inside which we hung on the hooks on the beams, as by this time the bacon racks had been taken down and put away. With no other light these looked quite spooky – why we didn't set the wooden beams on fire with them I don't know – God was obviously on our side.

We children went to bed early and hung our stockings on The Room mantlepiece. Dad was no flannel foot and hadn't a hope of creeping undetected into our bedroom so he didn't even try. On Christmas morning he got up first, did the milking and then lit the kitchen fire, after which he put the wireless (a battery set) on the bottom stairs and turned up the volume so that one and all were blasted out of bed by the sound of Christmas Carols. Of course we needed no urging, we just flung on our clothes in a haphazard fashion and dashed down to inspect our stockings. Mum would forbid us to open them before we'd had a token wash from the tin bowl on the kitchen sink and had shown our teeth the brush.

We always had walnuts, apples and oranges in our stockings, pencils, sharpeners, gloves and one other present. The year the boys had pocket knives I was utterly disgusted to get a large celluloid doll. Mother had knitted clothes for it and gone to a lot of trouble – so I must have hurt and disappointed her by my reception of it. Children can be cruel. We never had presents from people out of the family and never gave presents to others – the money simply was not there – and Mum and Dad had only a token present from each other. Therefore when one Christmas, never to be forgotten, a large parcel arrived for us, we were beside ourselves with excitement and delight. We all gathered round for a ceremonial opening – I had a chocolate violin and there was a box of sweets for each of the boys – also a lovely feather eiderdown each – sheer luxury and bliss. These were from an Aunt who lived in London. She had recently married a Police Superintendent as his second wife and decided to spread some of her good fortune round the family – dear, kind, beautiful Auntie Nellie. She didn't live long to enjoy her good fortune.

Dad usually gave himself a holiday at Christmas. After the morning milking all he did was a couple of hours yard work, i.e., feeding the animals, then the afternoon milking and that was that. Uncle and his family came in the afternoon by pony and trap and we all settled down to an enormous tea followed by party games, like hide the thimble, turn the trencher and forfeits, and postman's knock. A good time was had by all, specially after they'd had their glass of sherry. Boxing Day was quite different – another day of light work so that all the men and boys could go shooting. Dad didn't have the shooting rights of the farm. However all the tenant farmers shot on Boxing Day, presuming their Lords and Masters were safely tucked away elsewhere.

One year Dad took pity on me and let me join the beaters to flush out the game for them to shoot. It was cold and wet and very soon the novelty wore off. It was no fun walking through fields of sodden kale reaching nearly to one's waist, the ploughed land was heavy and sticky and difficult to cross. Dinner time couldn't come quickly enough for me – one more covert to draw and then food! We entered the last plantation, the guns were in position – my brothers, cousins and the lone girl were in position – we sloshed our way through the water-logged ground and then, suddenly, I tripped over a rotten branch lying half submerged in the mud. I said: 'B***** me!' Dad dropped his gun in surprise – it went off and narrowly missed a beater – everyone curled up in hysterical laughter – probably because the shot had missed everyone! The boys laughed themselves silly as I picked myself out of the mire. Dad said not a word.

92.

At our supper of cold meat and pickles with trifle and mince pies to follow Dad suddenly put down his knife and fork, looked sorrowfully at me and said: 'I didn't know my daughter knew such words.' It was the only reference he made to the incident – but there were generations of Methodism in his soul when he spoke. My brothers could have told him where his daughter had picked them up.

10.

3RD SEPTEMBER 1939 AND THE WAR YEARS

3RD SEPTEMBER 1939

I T WAS A GOD-GIVEN DAY. The morning sun gleamed with a sparkling freshness, not having been there long enough to get dusty. Hens and ducks clucked and quacked contentedly as they foraged around the yard where wheat and barley nestled among the dry cart-ruts, dropped from the harvest waggons the day before. It should have been a lovely day.

My dad stretched out his hand, hesitated a long moment as if he didn't want to know, then he turned the knob of the wireless set. My brothers and I were grouped around in dry silence, waiting for a new experience. My mother was sitting well apart from us by the fireside where the Sunday joint sizzled in the side-oven as if she already needed the extra comfort and warmth to see her through the long, hard worrying days ahead. She already had the experience and sorrow denied to the rest of us.

The voice, crackling a little before the set was properly tuned, gathered strength and clarity as the fateful words were uttered, ' . . . consequently, we are at war with Germany.'

It should have been a beautiful, summer Sunday but it was not. Already my two teenage brothers had a sheen of guilty excitement on their faces, looks of understanding passed between them. I was excluded from their silent communications; the females had always to play the passive roles. In their untried ignorance they were fired with patriotism, seeing only the adventure and daring, and none of the useless squalidness, the futility of any war – in their innocence not realising that everyone on both sides had to be the losers.

After such a momentous Sunday, the whole family retired to bed wondering what the future would bring. We hadn't long to wait. We all heard the unearthly wail of the siren sounding miles away in Sleaford . . . a moment's silence and then—uproar! Dad yelling to everyone to get up and get dressed; Mother trying to calm everyone down, pointing out that we'd be very unlucky if Hitler had picked on our farm for his very first raid. After a short interval we were shepherded outside into the Home Field while Dad picked a suitable safe spot for us all—the very centre of the 20 acre pasture. Here we settled back on the damp grass, the bright moonlight allowing us to inspect one another's selection of clothing. Suddenly Ray roared with laughter and pointed at me, the others followed suit. I couldn't see why I should be the source of such merriment; after all, I had done the right thing: I had put my gas-mask on first of all, and kept it on—in the middle of an enormous deserted field?

As the war got under way the countryside became organised to repel invasion. Ray began talking about joining the Navy as soon as he'd had his eighteenth birthday. Frank decided to join the Local Defence Volunteers, the LDV (later the Home Guard) or as we irreverently called them, the 'Look, Duck and Vanish' brigade.

For my Dad, the ultimate accolade – he was appointed the Captain, no less, of the local Auxiliary Fire Service, the AFS. He had two henchmen to assist him man the stirrup pump; one a large, strong young man, the other thin, tiny, frail, and elderly. The contrast had to be seen to be appreciated.

Dad assembled his troops on Sunday mornings for training. How many ways were there of using a stirrup pump? Greater scope was offered when they realised they were expected to rescue people from burning buildings: Dad had a simple answer – Go up the ladder to collect the one in danger; hoist them across the shoulders like a sack of corn, then descend the ladder. Yes, simple, but not when little Len had to carry big Walt, or my Dad who weighed a respectable thirteen and a half stones. Len just buckled at the knees, gave an apologetic smile to one and all and said: 'Not me, Maister! Oi'll look after t'pump'.

Of course, Frank and I gathered to watch all their antics, make helpful suggestions and ribald remarks. We had much fun at Dad's expense as, for some unknown reason, he always got the abbreviation wrong and claimed he was in charge of the local ATS! Now, to the best of our knowledge, there were no Women's Army personnel in the vicinity, so why this Freudian slip? Was it wishful thinking we wondered, or had he had a misspent middle age? Anyway, much to Mother's disapproval, he was always a 'Captain of the ATS'.

Civilians were involved in this War as never before, and we were no exceptions. One morning, my Dad went down the Levels to shepherd and found German incendiary bombs scattered all over the fields. Some had burnt themselves out but many more had not ignited. As we didn't want the stock to come to harm we collected all of them and stacked them in a big pile in the wash-house which was joined to the end of the farmhouse. Mother remonstrated about this but as Dad said, with unassailable logic, that if they hadn't exploded upon hitting the ground with great force then nothing we were likely to do would upset them. . . . To the best of my recollection the bombs stayed there for several weeks until Dad remembered (in his capacity as Chief of the AFS) to report their whereabouts. The Army then descended upon the farmyard with their lorry, complete with sand in the bottom, to remove them. As Dad, with the help of Frank and I, threw them with gusto into the back of the lorry the soldiers looked on apprehensively from a safe distance. My Uncle Sid, at Ewerby, was not so lucky. One night when everyone was abed, his housekeeper thought she heard an odd noise—'a wooshing', she said. She banged on Uncle's bedroom door and shouted out: 'Get up, we're being bombed!'

'Don't be daft, woman! Go back to bed! Who'd want to bomb us?' Thus discouraged, she did indeed return to her slumbers, but when the curtains were drawn in the morning, they found they had indeed been bombed. A string of high explosives had fallen across the farm buildings and dairy, and flattened the lot. As the crewyards were full of soft manure, the shock waves of the explosions had been absorbed, and the house, some seventy five yards away, had suffered no damage whatsoever. Unfortunately, most of the dairy herd were killed as were the calves in the nearby calf boxes. We supposed the German bombers had been looking for Cranwell.

One never-to-be-forgotten Sunday morning we were nearly ready to settle down to Sunday dinner when there burst upon us an enormous noise of aircraft engines. We dashed outside and then cowered down as a German bomber roared over us at fifty feet, or so it seemed, for it was low enough for us to see the two men in the cockpit very clearly. As they disappeared over the hedges our kitchen chimney, weakened earlier by a lightning strike, gave a creak and slowly keeled over into the garden – the downdraught from the aircraft we presumed.

Mother promptly had hysterics. 'I've got a white apron on – they could have seen me – they could have killed me!' she howled. A few minutes later we heard dull thuds, and learned afterwards that a house at Chapel Hill had been destroyed by a direct hit.

As I grew older the more work I was able to undertake on the farm. One job I hated was pumping buckets of water to carry to the 'cow-house' for swilling off the floor after milking. We always ended with wet feet or 'wetchered' as we called it. Another hateful task was churning the cream on butter-making days. I always tried to disappear but was usually run to earth and given the unenviable task. On cold winter days the butter usually came fairly quickly but on hot, sultry days I would turn that churn handle for what seemed like hours – my arms were practically dropping off by the time the cream co-operated and became butter. I was quite convinced I'd be permanently deformed by this task having one arm inches longer than the other.

As soon as brother Ray was old enough he joined the Fleet Air Arm, and I was promoted up the labour ladder. More responsible tasks fell to my lot. Now no one in their right mind would call me a natural driver: horses, yes, but anything with an engine . . . No!

One day my Dad decided it was high time I learnt to drive a tractor. Labour was in short supply and no doubt he had visions of me taking a man's place—eventually. So every spare minute during the school holidays I was badgered to have a go. Everyone told me how easy it was. 'Why, that owd Fordson's a little lady – she practically drives herself!' Don't you believe it – not for me she didn't.

After much persuasion, I agreed. Dad started the Fordson, hoisted me on to the cold, iron seat, pointed out to me what to pull and push, and told me to try going around the stackyard until I got the feel of things. This I proceeded to do under his eagle eye – to our mutual satisfaction and surprise. He then left me to it and went off to another job of work. I chugged round the stacks in the yard, went beside the barn, round the stacks a different way, then wove figures of eight to vary the route. Faster I went, then slower, until even I felt master of the machine. Now I was beginning to feel hungry so decided it was time to stop. I looked round for Dad to instruct me in the delicate art of stopping an internal combustion engine—no Dad. In fact, he'd forgotten all about me and gone for his dinner.

I yelled to him for help but no sign of Dad. I contemplated jumping off and leaving the wretched tractor to its own devices; I decided against this however—it would be cowardice. I kept on chugging round the stacks getting more and more desperate. Still no Dad. I called for him until I was hoarse. I pulled and pushed everything to hand; even the tractor seemed to be going faster to torment me. Then I had an inspiration: a sure and certain way of stopping floated into my mind; hang the consequences! I would do it . . . I drove the tractor straight into the side of the biggest stack in the yard. We came to a shuddering halt. I jumped off and didn't stop running until I reached the kitchen door. There was Dad peacefully tucking into his second helping of pudding. I had great satisfaction in telling him what I'd done. I had never seen him move so quickly . . . 'You'll have set the danged stackyard on fire,' he snarled as he ran. Luckily the Gods of wheat and barley were on my side that day.

At that point, brother Frank decided to take a hand in my driving education. He tucked me into his little Morris 8 Tourer. We scrunched our way over the Home field, through the beck until the steam rose from the engine, back round the curious cows and calves and came to a triumphant stop. 'There you are', said Frank, 'it's easy!' So the next time Dad wasn't looking we 'borrowed' a little agricultural petrol topped up with paraffin, and decided I should go solo. Full of confidence by now I pottered around the field again, round the dreaded stackyard and along by the barn. Frank yelled more instructions to me. As I couldn't hear clearly I turned round to look at him thereby turning the steering wheel . . . I careered over a parked plough and buried the bonnet of the little car in the barn wall. After this episode I wasn't asked to drive again for some time.

But time heals all wounds and blunts the memory, so during the following harvest – just after my fifteenth birthday – I was asked to go into Sleaford to Fenton & Townsend to fetch some replacement parts for the binder. 'How do I get there?' I asked.

Dad looked at me in surprise: 'In the car, of course!'

Obviously in the heat of the harvest moment he'd forgotten my previous escapades. 'It's easy to drive – come here, I'll show you.' So he did. I did remember to ask how to stop and start again, and as it seemed such a simple exercise I felt there was nothing to fear: no thoughts of licences or insurance entered our heads. Having ascertained precisely what spare parts I wanted, I set off. Suffice it to say the roads were empty of traffic and I arrived at Fentons safely; indeed, triumphantly. I drew in with a flourish and parked the car as near to the door as I could.

Transactions complete, I put the parts on the back seat of the car and climbed nonchalantly into the driver's seat. I pulled the starter and the engine burst into life. I looked at the diagram on the top of the gear lever and found nothing that said 'Backwards'. I depressed the clutch very slowly and engaged a gear I thought I hadn't used before: my mistake, I had! The car gave a kangaroo leap forward and coyly pushed open the shop door. The engine stalled: I was quite pleased about this as I didn't actually want to drive to the counter to ask for help. Much leg-pulling and ribaldry later, one of the men reversed the car and parked it back on the road, pointing in the right direction. I drove off to a resounding cheer.

As I didn't confess this little episode at home, everyone

thought I had mastered the art of driving. I did take the precaution of watching closely when Dad or Frank reversed the car and soon believed that I had it all under control. When, a week or two later, Mother asked me to drive to Sleaford to take some plums and apples to her friend, Mrs Drury, I was full of confidence.

I swept through Sleaford, up Grantham Road and parked with a flourish in the Drury drive. Mother's commission duly completed, I began to reverse the car back onto the main road. Now all would have been well if the drive had been wider, or at least the gateway had been wider. With the steering wheel behind you when you are peering over your shoulder proves a tricky situation – as I realised when I'd flattened the left hand gatepost. Mrs Drury wasn't pleased – I didn't blame her. I carefully eased the car forward and changed into reverse again. This time I looked over the other shoulder, determined to give the flattened post a wide berth. In this I succeeded but uprooted the right hand post in the process. This time Mrs Drury was frantic and shouted, 'Just go . . . my husband will put them back . . . just go!'

Mother was not amused as she felt she couldn't charge for the plums and apples: Dad roared with laughter, and brother Frank took me in hand and made a decent driver of me. A year later I bought a provisional licence.

The War, of course, made an impact on our lives in other ways. We had better food than most people – even though our diet was the same as it had always been – the difference being that people in the towns relied on rationed goods alone; people in the countryside supplemented their diet in many ways.

Now very short of labour, we had the mixed blessing of three Land Army girls. One, Jackie, was beautiful, great fun and a good worker; the other two just the opposite. They were both from the East End of London and all they wanted was to be sent back. It wasn't their fault they felt like fish out of water and I suppose, after the first skirmish over House Rules, we didn't exactly help. They called my mother 'Maria Monk' and all their mail came addressed 'c/o M. Monk'. They soon attained their objective— back to London they went.

Our next labour came in the form of Prisoners of War. They were billeted in Ewerby and every morning Frank fetched four of them in the car for the day's work. No one even thought they might try to escape! One, a farmer from Westphalia, was a great asset; the others were good fun and good workers. Two were college students and spoke passable English; it made their day if they could find any excuse to get into the farm kitchen and Mother, against all the rules, gave them cups of tea.

As the months dragged on we admitted that, as a family, we were quite puzzled. Of course we had our friends amongst the farming fraternity; Frank and I had school friends and acquaintances for miles around, as did everyone in the country – but why were we so popular? People were going out of their way to speak to us – people we hardly knew. Enlightenment arrived one day in the form of a local doctor who drove into the yard to see if we were all fit; had we escaped the heavy colds that were going the rounds? Then he tentatively asked Mother if she could spare him half a dozen eggs! The mystery was solved: it wasn't our spirited conversation they were after – it was our produce! Apparently Mother had established a small but flourishing black market . . .

Cast in the role of courier, on the way to school I would deliver an occasional half pound of butter; half dozens of eggs here and there; fruit in summer, sometimes a chicken or two, and after pig-killing a few sausages were known to change hands. Of course, we always had just a little left over the odds and suddenly, for the very first time in our lives money was slightly easier to come by. Now and then, a fresh piece of furniture would appear in the house— to my dad's total surprise. When questioned, my Mother would answer airily: 'The eggs were a good price this week and the . . . er . . . rabbits made good money too.' . . . Poor Dad! he never suspected that his patient, hardworking, long-suffering wife was up to her neck in trade. He, who wouldn't let even a drop of agricultural petrol find its way into the tanks of the car, was completely hoodwinked.

Every so often, an auction was held in Sleaford Market. 'Spitfire Sales' they were called. People donated unwanted items and the resultant cash went towards the cost of a Spitfire.

101.

Mother could now attend with real purpose. Perhaps her greatest triumph was the acquisition of a beautiful grandfather clock by W. Read of Grantham, circa 1790, for the princely sum of One Pound, Ten Shillings! Dad was even more mystified: he knew his wife could work a good bargain but this was ridiculous. Frank and I enjoyed to the full this marital by-play— in complete silence, of course!

Our chief personal worry, however, was the safety of brother Ray. He completed his initial training aboard HMS Royal Arthur (as Butlins holiday camp became for the duration) at Skegness. On his first leave, complete in bell-bottoms and square-rig uniform, this gallant lad looked quite a sight. None of us had ever seen a better crop of boils anywhere, totally spoiling his dashing apperance. There they were, on chin, neck, chest, absolutely throbbing with venom. We felt so sorry for him but he assured us they were easy to be rid of: all one had to do was heat a pan of water and when very hot place into the water the neck of a fairly large bottle. When this was heated, remove from the pan and put the neck over one of the boils and it would pull out all the contained matter. Mother, hovering around with antiseptic ointments, was horrified. Frank and I watched, fascinated. However successful this remedy proved by itself, I do not know; it certainly looked painful. The final solution was probably a mixture of both remedies.

As the months rolled by and the war ebbed and flowed, we listened to the news broadcasts on the wireless with constant attention. The bulletin that told us about the 'Thousand Bomber' raid on Germany came as no surprise. Situated as we were in the middle of what became known as Bomber County, it was obvious to us that the war in the air was an all-out effort. Frank and I sat on the gate into the Home Field night after night counting the squadrons of aircraft, the Lancasters, Halifaxes, Wellingtons, and Stirlings as they flew over towards their targets in the night skies. It seemed to take hours for the streams of bombers to disappear over the south-eastern horizon. Then, during the early hours of the morning, we could hear the constant drone of the returning aircraft. We would peer from the bedroom windows and try to count them back home again – like shepherds with their flocks. Quite often we heard the sound of an aircraft in difficulties – we could always tell – the uneven beat as they passed overhead, and they took with them our prayers that they would make it back to base or a diversionary airfield.

In one early dawn we heard a plane in great distress – low and faltering – then dead silence until we heard a 'Crummph'. Soon we were out in the fields looking for it, but we weren't the first on the scene: it had crashed on the neighbouring farm and to the delight of all around it was found to be a German bomber. Apparently the crew had baled out and been captured.

One night, after many bombers had passed over on their way to the continent and all was quiet, we heard a most unusual noise – pebbles on the windows it seemed. Had we been invaded? Dad grabbed his 12–bore gun and very quietly we opened the black-out over the back door and peered out. A large black shape stood there; 'Who is it?' demanded my father, gun barrels jutting aggressively into the night. 'Don't you know your own son?' said my brother Ray's voice, quietly. Mother cried with delight as we all piled downstairs and had a real party. Ray had just returned from India; his ship had stopped at the Cape for repairs. There he'd seen natives walking on white hot stones; in India he'd seen the Indian rope-trick and the Taj Mahal by moonlight; he'd been on Malta when they'd bombed it day and night. . . . We realised he was exhausted and soon fast asleep. We crept up to bed again: we'd seen Ray.

His leaves were all too short and infrequent; his letters home were censored. Mother wrote to him every Sunday evening for five and a half years, without fail. However tired she was, she always made time for that.

POSTSCRIPT

While all this was happening, I was growing older. School Certificate came and went, and I had to make a choice. Should I stay and help on the farm, or further my education? My Dad agreed with me that I should continue my studies.

That decision marked the end of a chapter in my life; my childhood on our Lincolnshire farm. It marked the beginning of a new chapter; new horizons, new friends. – I went to college.

a new chapter; new horizons, new friends. — I went to college.

* * * * *

Dad lived until his 88th year. He never retired, he just became slower and did less work, and left the decision-making to my brother Frank who took over the farm from him.

The incidents of childhood are seen through the eyes of children; we appreciate our parents, relations and friends with childish frivolity and affection. This much, I think, springs from these pages. Only much later did we see what was really there – when we had the maturity to see it.

When my Dad spoke of wanting to become a teacher of history, I think with hindsight he was trying to encourage me. He would not have been happy anywhere but on his farm: for him the earth was good and he was the custodian of his acres. They were not his, they were in his keeping; the crops, the cattle, the sheep were his to nurture as best he could. He strove not just to make a living, important though that was, but to do so with respect for the land.

My Dad never lived anywhere but on a farm; he never left it for longer than a few days at a time, until a heart attack forced him into a hospital.

He and my mother gave us a very happy childhood: this little book is in their memory.